MODERN CLAVICHORD MUSIC

Francis Knights

Peacock Press

Modern Clavichord Music, Francis Knights
Copyright © 2024

The right of Francis Knights to be identified as the Author of the Work has been asserted by him in accordance with the Copyright, Designs and Patents Act 1988.

All rights reserved. No part of this publication may be reproduced, stored in a retrieval system or transmitted in any form or by any means electronic, mechanical, photocopying, recording or otherwise, without the prior written permission of the author.

Published by Peacock Press,
Scout Bottom Farm, Mytholmroyd,
Hebden Bridge,
West Yorkshire
HX7 5JS,
United Kingdom

ISBN 978-1-914934-93-3

Designed by DM Design and Print

Cover: Unfretted clavichord by Peter Owen (photo: Beatrice Heslop), by kind permission.

MODERN CLAVICHORD MUSIC

Francis Knights

CONTENTS

Acknowledgements	p.ii
Preface	p.1
1. Introduction	p.3
2. The Clavichord Revival	p.11
3. Performers, Concerts and Recordings	p.31
4. Creating a Repertoire	p.41
5. A century of Clavichord Music	p.47
6. A Guide to Composing for the Clavichord	p.59
7. Performing the Clavichord Repertoire	p.67
Catalogue of Works	p.73
Select Discography	p.125
Bibliography	p.133
Index	p.151

In memory of composer
Ivan Moody (1964-2024)

ACKNOWLEDGEMENTS

My thanks go to the numerous composers, performers, publishers and collectors who have kindly supplied scores and recordings over the past forty years, in particular Joan Benson, David Bohn, David Loeb, Anna Maria McElwain and Michael Thomas. Thanks are also due to the many composers who have responded to my requests for new works for the clavichord (the very first of whom was my friend Ivan Moody, to whom this book is dedicated), and to Peter Bavington, Julia Seiber Boyd, Jeremy Burbage, Sarah MacDonald, Peter Owen, Pablo Padilla and Lavern Wagner for other assistance, information or support.

Many of the scores listed in the Catalogue below have been collected by the author, and may be consulted by scholars on request;* generally, those works where the compass is indicated are available. Recordings are listed separately in my published *Clavichord Discography*, and some of these can also be made available.

Francis Knights

Cambridge
July 2024

* For contact details, see www.francisknights.co.uk.

PREFACE

The contemporary clavichord repertoire has its origins in a paradox: the rediscovery of the instrument, as part of the wider early music revival, initially came about as a reaction to several features of late 19th century music and society: a noisy industrial and mechanized world; Romantic excesses of musical volume and scale; and the anguished dissonances of modern music. The clavichord seemed an ideal antidote to all this modernity, and its repertoire – from the exuberance of the virginalists to the elegance of the classical style – a return to an ordered musical civilization. The very idea of using it as a tool for contemporary music is therefore surprising in some ways, so the gentleness of the modernity exemplified by Herbert Howells' seminal post-Tudor set *Lambert's Clavichord* of 1928 was probably critical to some of the success of what followed. As Richard Terry wrote in a review of that volume, 'Sooner or later it was bound to come that some modern English composer would set himself or herself to write music for these resuscitated instruments of the past. The danger would have been considerable, had the first attempts been more imitations of the old idiom'.[1]

Compositions for the clavichord in the early 20th century depended on the availability of both working instruments and interested performers, and the narrative of the clavichord revival (Chapter 2) and its performers (Chapter 3), and the means by which these elements came together (Chapter 4), takes the view that musical serendipity had a important part to play. How many clavichords existed, where they were located, what was played on them, and by whom, is less important than the circumstances in which an individual composer might hear a concert or broadcast that stimulated an idea for a work, happened across an instrument or maker, wrote for a clavichord they owned themselves, or met a performer looking (or not) for

---

1 Richard Runciman Terry, [Review of Lambert's Clavichord], *The Spectator* (7 November 1928).

new repertoire. This is partly because the normal compositional outcomes for (say) the equivalent harpsichord repertoire – a public recital, a recording or a publication – do not apply to the clavichord in the same way. Nor was there a repertoire – such as the major 20th century harpsichord concertos – to follow as a model, and thus contribute to a known tradition. Nevertheless, the clavichord offered novelty of sound, and some unique characteristics such as *bebung* (finger vibrato), thus new compositions attracted adventurous performers looking for more dissonant and exciting repertoire; as with the harpsichord, some contemporary music specialists emerged, while others commissioned or performed new works occasionally.

The development of the modern clavichord repertoire is explored in Chapter 5, taking first Britain – whose particular musical and stylistic characteristics owe much to the instrument makers there and to neoclassical and pastoral traditions – then the US, and Europe. While some recent Calls for Scores have brought in interesting new composers from further afield, including Latin America, Eastern Europe and Asia, the performing tradition for new clavichord repertoire is still mainly focused on the US and Britain – for now. By way of encouragement, practical advice is offered for composers (Chapter 6) and for performers (Chapter 7) – it is clear that personal relationships between the two parties have much to do with the successful creation of new repertoire, and it is important for both sides to understand each other.

The detailed Catalogue is supported by a Select Discography and an extensive Bibliography. Referencing throughout has been thorough, as (for example) three key documentary sources, the *De Clavicordo* Magnano conference proceedings, the journal *Clavichord International* and the *British Clavichord Society Newsletter*, are available only in print form, and not widely available, the proceedings series having ended and the other two periodicals ceased publication.

CHAPTER 1

INTRODUCTION

The clavichord, as an affordable, quiet, and portable keyboard instrument for individual study, had an important role in domestic European music from the 16th to the 18th centuries in many countries. The early music movement, begun in the late 19th century,[2] saw an important symbolic role for the revived clavichord as an emblem of past music thanks to the advocacy of Arnold Dolmetsch (1858–1940) and his supporters, but actual instruments were not widely available for many decades, and were also relatively slow to appear on recordings.[3] In some sense the instrument did not even need 'reviving', as it never quite died out: the Dolmetsch family not only continued playing the clavichord at home during the 19th century, but it was used as a practice instrument in the Zurich music school founded by Bachophile Friedrich Dolmetsch (1782-1861). There, the children practiced clavichords 'in different corners of the same room, without hearing each other', as reported by Carl Dolmetsch (1911-1997) from his great-aunt Aline (born in about 1835); the repertoire included 'Bach's preludes and fugues'.[4]

The musical tradition begins

The earliest 20th century work for the clavichord was thought to be Herbert

---

[2] For the background, see Joel Cohen and Herb Snitzer, *Reprise: The Extraordinary Revival of Early Music* (Boston: Little, Brown, 1985), Harry Haskell, *The Early Music Revival: A History* (London: Thames and Hudson, 1988) and Nick Wilson, *The Art of Re-enchantment: Making Early Music in the Modern Age* (Oxford: Oxford University Press, 2014).

[3] Francis Knights, *Clavichord Discography* (Hebden Bridge: Peacock Press, 2020).

[4] Kenneth Mobbs, 'The BCS at Haslemere, September 1995: the work of Arnold Dolmetsch', *British Clavichord Society Newsletter*, 4 (February 1996), pp.11-13 at 11; John Weston, 'George Bernard Shaw and the Clavichord: Part 3', *British Clavichord Society Newsletter*, 19 (February 2001), pp.15-18 at 15.

Howells' 'Lambert's Fireside', dated 14 May 1926 and literally composed at Herbert Lambert's fireside near Bath; this became the first piece in *Lambert's Clavichord*, Op.41 (1928).[5] However, there are documentary records of two other unpublished earlier pieces involving clavichord by German composers, neither of which appears to survive. In 1913 Walter Niemann (1876-1953) wrote *Westminster, Eine kleine Hausmusik nach William Byrd* for violin, cello, clavichord and glockenspiel. Aside from this very unusual scoring, one wonders where Niemann might have found a working clavichord at A440, it being unlikely that he then either had access to an original instrument at that pitch, or any kind of early revival copy.[6] Niemann would certainly have known about the instrument, however, having published a successful history of the keyboard entitled *Das Klavierbuch* (1907),[7] and while most of his extensive range of piano compositions are in full late-Romantic style, his set of three Sonatinas, Op.24 'für pianoforte' (perhaps significantly, also dating from 1913) do not require the sustaining pedal and are easily adjusted to lie within the clavichord's compass. It is therefore entirely possible that *Westminster* was a genuine clavichord chamber work. The other early non-survivor is a Suite in A minor (1903-25) for harpsichord or clavichord by composer and musicologist Walter Harburger (1887-1967); the wide composition date range is curious, but nothing more is known, except that one contemporary source described it as being in 'the old style'.[8]

Literary connections

The clavichord revival emerged as part of the English 'Arts and Crafts'

---

5   The remaining works are dated from London between 19 July and 10 September 1927.

6   He is not listed as an owner, for example, in Donald Boalch, rev. Charles Mould, *Makers of the Harpsichord and Clavichord* (Oxford: Oxford University Press, 3/1995), now updated online at https://boalch.org.

7   Walter Niemann, *Das Klavierbuch, kurze Geschichte d. Klaviermusik u. ihrer Meister, d. Klavierbaues u. d. Klavierliteratur* (Munich: Callwey Verlag, 1907). In 1919 he also published a book on virginal music.

8   *Enciclopedia universal ilustrada europeo-americana*, xxvii (Madrid: Espasa-Calpe S.A., 1908-1930), p.674.

movement,[9] and therefore had strong links with literary and artistic traditions of the period. Poets and writers who owned an instrument included Robert Bridges (1844–1930), George Bernard Shaw (1856–1950) and Ezra Pound (1885–1972), together with (probably) the painter Raoul Dufy (1877–1953).[10] Pound wrote in 1915, 'So here I am with a clavichord – beside me, which I can't afford and can't reasonably play on', but kept the instrument all his life.[11] This musical and social mix of the intelligentsia and the aristocracy also included Lord Berners (1883-1950), who owned a Dolmetsch clavichord (1921/22) which had a special storage space in his chauffeur-driven Rolls-Royce; this may well be of the 'travelling' fretted variety that Dolmetsch occasionally produced, as in No.107 of 1933, with a compass of C-d^3 and length of only 86 cm.[12] Given Berners (professionally, Gerald Tyrwhitt) was a noted composer (as well as novelist and painter), it is a pity that he does not appear to have written specifically for the instrument.

The clavichord was also mentioned in poetry, such as the short set of verses called 'The Clavichord' (1907) by Dollie Radford (1858-1920), which must have been the result of her hearing a Dolmetsch instrument, and its 'sweet whisperings in the air'.[13] The clavichord is also mentioned in poems

---

9   Derek Adlam, 'Arts and Crafts and the Clavichord, The Revival of Early Instrument Building in England', in Bernard Brauchli, Susan Brauchli and Alberto Galazzo (eds.), *De Clavicordio II*, Proceedings of the International Clavichord Symposium (Turin: Musica Antica a Magnano, 1995), pp.201-212; Larry Palmer, 'Some Literary References to the Harpsichord and Clavichord, 1855-1923', *Diapason*, lxxiv (September 1983), p.18; Edmond Johnson, 'The Death and Second Life of the Harpsichord', *The Journal of Musicology*, xxx/2 (Spring 2013), pp.180-214.

10   Peter Bavington, 'Thomas Goff and his Clavichords', *British Clavichord Society Newsletter*, 16 (February 2000), pp.7-11 at 10.

11   Forrest Read (ed.), *Pound/Joyce: The Letters of Ezra Pound to James Joyce with Pound's Essays on Joyce* (New York: New Directions, 1967), p.46.

12   Uta Henning, 'Arnold Dolmetsch and his Bach Clavichord: an Iconographical and Literary Approach', in Bernard Brauchli, Alberto Galazzo and Judith Wardman (eds.), *De Clavicordio VIII*, Proceedings of the International Clavichord Symposium (Magnano: Musica Antica a Magnano, 2008), pp.17-26 at 25; Tim Hamilton, 'A Very Small Dolmetsch', *Tangents*, 18 (Spring 2005), pp.4-5.

13   From Dollie Radford, *A Ballad of Victory and other Poems* (London: Alston Rivers, 1907), and reproduced in the *British Clavichord Society Newsletter*, 5 (June 1996), p.36.

by Robert Bridges (1844-1930), Thomas Hardy (1840-1928), Walter de la Mare (1873-1956) and Ezra Pound, and by W. H. Gerry in the US. How well the latter understood the instrument's exact mechanism is in doubt, as he writes in 1937 of 'myriad frail hammers'. The clavichord began to appear in novels in the early 20th century, as writers came across it, either in person or at second hand: for example, a clavichord performance is described in John Galsworthy's *The Silver Spoon* (1926).[14] All these literary references - Dolmetsch himself was fictionalized in George Moore's *Evelyn Innes* (1898) - together with the early keyboard composers mentioned in novels such as James Joyce's *Ulysses* (1922), would have helped the wider public to hear about the clavichord, and early music more generally.[15]

Also moving in these British cultural circles were the Sitwells, Osbert and Edith, both admirers of clavichordist Violet Gordon Woodhouse; for six years after her death, they put the John Milton quotation, 'Time will run back, and fetch the age of gold' in an anniversary notice in *The Times*. It was the lid motto on an instrument Thomas Goff had made for her in 1946.[16]

Instrument types

While the simple design of the clavichord prevents any major restructural thinking, there have been a number of interpretations in modern times,[17] some of which have been used by composers. The firm of Edelan has constructed an aluminum clavichord, which has an appropriately metallic tone,[18] while Carl Dudash has created an upright clavichord, as a parallel

---

14 Joan Benson, 'Clavichord Perspectives from Goethe to Pound', in Bernard Brauchli, Alberto Galazzo and Ivan Moody (eds.), *De Clavicordio VI*, Proceedings of the International Clavichord Symposium (Magnano: Musica Antica a Magnano, 2004), pp.139-147.

15 Francis Knights, 'Early Music in the Novel', *Dolmetsch Foundation Bulletin*, New Series No.40 (Autumn 2021), pp.9-11.

16 Chau-Yee Lo, *Endangered Species: The Harpsichord and its New Repertoire since 1960*, PhD thesis (University of Leeds, 2004), pp.37-38.

17 See, for example, R. A. Hands, 'A Scientific Approach to the Clavichord', *The Galpin Society Journal*, xx (March 1967), pp.89-98.

18 https://myemail.constantcontact.com/The-edelan-6061-Aluminum-Clavichord.html?soid= 1105784870832&aid=6n4qQS-tLjA (accessed January 18, 2022).

to the upright harpsichord or *clavicytherium* occasionally made in the 18th century and earlier.[19] One 18th-century innovation, the sound-altering stops of the pantalon clavichord, has not yet made it into the modern repertory.[20] Nor have two other historical variants: adding a separate pedalboard to the instrument to enable organ practice domestically;[21] while the cembal d'amour designed by Gottfried Silbermann divided each string in the middle at the tangent contact point, leading to a very long instrument. This rare design has been reconstructed in modern times by Hugh Gough, Sean Rawnsley/ Michael Thomas, Merzdorf, Lyndon Johann Taylor and Ed Mauger.[22]

The most common historical variant was the fretted clavichord, where several keys shared one pair of strings, the brass tangents carefully spaced to produce two, three or four semitones (thus double-, triple- or quadruple-fretted). This resulted in a narrow string-band, simpler construction and lower cost, and was very common until the second half of the 18th century, where the performance restrictions began to conflict with wider harmonic exploration by composers – only one note can be played at a time on each string. The last known such instrument was a five-octave clavichord by Klemens Kunz of Jaroma (1839), which by then would have seemed very old-fashioned indeed. As the writings of collector Carl Engel (1818-1882) indicate, this design was virtually unknown by the end of the 19th century,[23] and so it was hardly part of the modern clavichord revival at all. However, some scholars were aware of it, and in the late 1920s Eric Blom showed that he understood the problems that fretting caused in performing Bach's

---

19   Carl Dudash, 'An Upright Clavichord', *Clavichord International*, xiii/1 (May 2009), pp.21-24.

20   Paul Simmonds, 'The Story of a Pantalon Clavichord', *Clavichord International*, xi/1 (May 2007), pp.22-26.

21   Susi Jeans, 'The Pedal Clavichord and Other Instruments of Organists', *Proceedings of the Royal Musical Association*, 77th session (1950–51), pp.1–15; Karrin Ford, 'The Pedal Clavichord and the Pedal Harpsichord', *The Galpin Society Journal*, l (1997), pp.161–179; Joel Speerstra, *Bach and the Pedal Clavichord: an Organist's Guide* (Rochester, NY: University of Rochester Press, 2004).

22   Lyndon Johann Taylor, 'Reconstructing Silbermann's Cembal d'Amour', *Clavichord International*, i/2 (November 1997), pp.43-45.

23   Paul Simmonds, 'Carl Engel and the Clavichord', *The Galpin Society Journal*, lxi (April 2008), pp.105-113 at 109.

Well-Tempered Clavier, in a way that suggests direct experience.[24] The turning point came well after the war, when Edwin Ripin pointed out that – for earlier repertoire especially – the simpler design did offer some advantages. Even for instruments from the 1780s, he polemically asserted that the double-fretted instruments were 'far more efficient, sensitive, and finer-toned musical instruments than their larger rivals'.[25] Once fretted historical copies became more widely available, a number of composers began to use them, and to explore the slightly different possibilities they offered (for example, striking an already-sounding string with the tangent of an adjacent key, producing a metallic clang); Alissa Duryee's *Forager's Journal* (2018) is an excellent example of writing for frets (ex.1.1). As with such specialist instruments, contemporary works for fretted clavichord cannot be played on unfretted clavichords (and vice versa), which does limit performance opportunities.

One historical (and modern) refinement which fretting makes possible is microtonality, with additional intervals smaller than a semitone. This has be done with keyboards since the 16th century, and is again in use,[26] with music by Heiner Ruland, Stefan Müller and Johann Sonnleitner. The modern microtonal clavichord uses an additional row of 12 'sharp' keys per octave at a slightly higher level, in a similar way to the historical enharmonic harpsichord; unlike that instrument, the quarter tones are achieved by fretting rather than needing additional strings. The first clavichord of this design was built by Fritz Lengemann in 1966, followed by three other makers. Again,

---

24   Eric Blom, 'Bach and the Clavier', *The Musical Times*, lxix/1019 (1 January 1928), pp.25-27. But note that Arnold Dolmetsch disagreed with his assessment of the problem: see Arnold Dolmetsch, *The Interpretation of The Music of the XVII and XVIII Centuries* (London: Novello and Co., 1916), p.435.

25   Edwin M. Ripin, 'A Reassessment of the Fretted Clavichord', *The Galpin Society Journal*, xxiii (August 1970), pp.40-48 at 45.

26   See Douglas Keislar, 'History and Principles of Microtonal Keyboards', *Computer Music Journal*, xi/1 (Spring 1987), pp.18-28.

works composed for such instruments offers new creative possibilities,[27] but cannot be played on any other type of clavichord.

Ex.1.1 Alissa Duryee, Forager's Journal, *p.3, by permission of the composer*

Lastly, electronics offer ways of amplifying or modifying clavichord tone. The normal way to do this is to insert a small microphone or pickup in or on the soundbox, which has been done effectively.[28] Renée Geoffrion has gone further, and designed an electro-acoustic clavichord,[29] for which Louis-Philippe Rivet's *Nomoi of the Great Olympian Divinities* (2006) was written,

---

27 See Johann Sonnleitner, 'The Clavichord in the Expanded Tone System', in Brauchli, Galazzo and Moody (2002), pp.63-71, Florian Sonnleitner, 'The Klavikantal - A new Type of Clavichord in Development', in Bernard Brauchli, Alberto Galazzo and Ivan Moody (eds.), *De Clavicordio V*, Proceedings of the International Clavichord Symposium (Magnano: Musica Antica a Magnano, 2002), pp.73-76 and Sally Fortino, 'Clavichord Music with Extended Tonality: a report from Switzerland', *British Clavichord Society Newsletter*, 53 (June 2012), pp.8-9.

28 Lyndon Johann Taylor, 'The Case for and against the Electric Clavichord', *British Clavichord Society Newsletter*, 8 (June 1997), pp.7-10.

29 Renée Geoffrion, 'The Electro-Acoustic Clavichord', *Tangents*, xvii (Fall 2004), pp.1, 5-6.

while the 'clavinet' electric instrument built by the Hohner company from 1964 to the 1980s was widely used in pop music.[30]

Cataloguing the repertoire

By the 1960s the modern repertoire for early keyboards had grown to such a size that it was becoming noticed: in 1963 Michael Steinberg, was able to list no fewer than 150 composers for the harpsichord,[31] and thirty years later Frances Bedford produced a substantial book cataloguing some 5,000 modern works (there are probably around 10,000 by now).[32] This included about a hundred and forty solo pieces for clavichord, a great expansion of the list of just 21 - mainly English - compiled by Lavern Wagner in 1969.[33] Most recently, Herbert Grundhewer and Lothar Bemmann produced a catalogue of several hundred works, but this was still partial.[34]

---

30 Huw Rees, 'The Hohner clavinet', *Clavichord International*, xvii/1 (May 2013), pp.6-13.

31 Michael Steinberg, 'Some Observations on the Harpsichord in Twentieth Century Music', *Perspectives of New Music*, i/2 (Spring 1963), pp.189-194.

32 Frances Bedford, *Harpsichord & Clavichord Music of the Twentieth Century* (Berkeley: Fallen Leaf Press, 1993). See also Frances Bedford, 'Twentieth Century Clavichord Music', in Susan Brauchli and Alberto Galazzo (eds.), *De Clavicordio* (Turin: Musica Antica a Magnano, 1994), pp.259-263; Rita Peiretti, 'Contemporary Clavichord Music in Italy', in Brauchli, Brauchli and Galazzo (1994), pp.265-266; Larry Palmer, 'Contemporary Harpsichord Music', in Mark Kroll (ed.), *The Cambridge Companion to the Harpsichord* (Cambridge: Cambridge University Press, 2019), pp.324-346; and Francis Knights, 'The evolution of modern clavichord music', in Rebecca Cypess, Esteli Gomez and Rachel Lansang (eds.), *Historical Performance and New Music: Aesthetics and Practices* (Abingdon, 2024), pp.106-117.

33 Lavern Wagner, 'The Clavichord Today, Part II', *Periodical of the Illinois State Music Teachers Association*, vii/1 (Summer 1969), pp.1-16.

34 Herbert Grundhewer and Lothar Bemmann, *Musik für Clavichord aus dem 20. und 21. Jahrhundert, Bibliografie* (Berlin: Deutschen Clavichord Societät, 2023).

CHAPTER 2

THE CLAVICHORD REVIVAL

The history of the harpsichord revival in modern times has been thoroughly studied,[35] but this is less true of the parallel clavichord revival.[36] This is in part because it is a different story, only partly involving the same performers, instrument makers – and composers. As Howard Schott noted many years ago, 'Who was playing what, where and upon which instruments is still incompletely understood'.[37]

The harpsichord revival

The death of the harpsichord at the hands of the piano in the Romantic era was slightly slower than might have been expected: both Gioacchino Rossini and Giuseppe Verdi were taught to play the harpsichord as children, despite growing up at a time when the instrument was already seen as outmoded.[38] And although there were a small number of instruments kept in working order during the 19th century and used for historical concerts and demonstration purposes, one real impetus for the revival of the craft

---

35 Raymond Russell, 'The Harpsichord since 1800', *Proceedings of the Royal Musical Association*, 82nd Session (1955-1956), pp.61-74; Zuckermann (1969); Howard Schott, 'The Harpsichord Revival', *Early Music*, ii/2 (April 1974), pp.85-95; Larry Palmer, *Harpsichord in America: A Twentieth Century Revival* (Bloomington, 1989); Edward L. Kottick, *A History of the Harpsichord* (Bloomington: Indiana University Press, 2003); Johnson (2013); Mark Kroll (ed.), *The Boston school of harpsichord building: reminiscences of William Dowd, Eric Herz and Frank Hubbard by the people who knew and worked with them* (Hillsdale, NY: Pendragon Press, 2019b).

36 John Barnes, 'The Parallel between the Harpsichord and Clavichord Revivals in the Twentieth Century', *De Clavicordio II* (1995), pp.234–240; Lothar Bemmann, 'The Decline and Revival of the Clavichord', in Brauchli, Galazzo and Moody (2004), pp.29-36.

37 Howard Schott 'From Harpsichord to Pianoforte: A Chronology and Commentary', *Early Music*, xiii/1 (February 1985), pp.28-38 at 28.

38 Kottick (2003), p.396.

skills needed to make a working instrument came from the Paris Exposition of 1889, where Tomasini, Érard and Pleyel all produced double manual harpsichords that owed much to the celebrated 1769 Taskin harpsichord, which was in playable condition and available as a model in France.[39] The idea of using the harpsichord for new music followed remarkably quickly, with the first new work - Francis Thomé's *Rigodon*, Op.97 - dating from from the mid-1890s.[40] A small number of solo works followed from composers like Busoni and Castelnuovo-Tedesco, as well as the instrument being used in orchestral scores, but the turning point came with its use as a concerto soloist, with notable works by De Falla (1926) and Poulenc (1929) written for Wanda Landowska, then a concerto by Martinů (1935) for Marcelle de Lacour. A combination of adventurous performers looking for exciting new harpsichord repertoire followed, but as relatively few of the leading recitalists of the inter-war period were interested in the clavichord (Ralph Kirkpatrick was a rare exception), partly because it could play no part in their paid concert work, it took a different path. Unhelpfully, Landowska herself was relatively hostile to the instrument.[41]

The antiquarian clavichord

In one respect, the clavichord had a major advantage over the harpsichord: the very simplicity of its design meant that keeping an old instrument working, or restoring one to some sort of playing order, often required little more than access to appropriate brass wire to keep it fully strung and sounding: as Dolmetsch explained to a workshop visitor: 'the clavichord any tuner can fix, or you can fix and tune it yourself if you have a good ear; it is quite simple'.[42]

Over a thousand historical clavichords have survived, about half of which

---

39 Kottick (2003), pp.409-414.
40 For the revival of the harpsichord, see Barnes (1995); Palmer (2019), pp.324–346 and Lo (2004).
41 Richard Troeger, 'Landowska and the Clavichord', *Harpsichord & Fortepiano*, xix/1 (Autumn 2014), pp.7–8.
42 Palmer (1989), p.22.

are anonymous.⁴³ Records of such clavichords which were used, repaired or restored in the 19th century make up a more extensive list than might have been expected: for example, one Slovakian teacher-training college used the instrument up until 1847, an 1810 Schmahl appears to have been in school use in Bavaria in 1874, while instruments were repaired throughout the 19th century for private owners (implying usage), museums and collectors.⁴⁴ In Frankfurt in 1839 a Silbermann clavichord was advertised as 'still good, very useful for an organist in the countryside'.⁴⁵ Late usage appears to have been focused on education and organists' practice – as had been the case in the Baroque. Collector Morris Steinert (1831-1912), who had clavichord lessons in Bavaria as a boy, later returned from the US, tracked down the instrument he had learnt on and bought the very same 1789 Schiedmayer, which is now in Boston.⁴⁶

A combination of musical and antiquarian impulses saw a number of Romantic and later composers collecting clavichords, some or all of which were in working order: Brahms owned an FF-g^3 instrument by Ferdinand Hoffman of about 1790 (now in Vienna), Mendelssohn owned a clavichord,⁴⁷ Liszt appears to have owned the 'ex-Mozart' Freiderici (destroyed in Vienna during WW2), Anton Bruckner used an instrument belonging to a local weaver Johann Sücka in the early 1840s for playing Bach and Albrechtberger,⁴⁸ while Carl Nielsen's own fretted clavichord (compass C-e^3, c.1730s German)

---

43 Boalch (1995) and http://www.clavichord.info/clavkult_literatur.html.

44 Bemmann (2004), pp.29-36.

45 Lothar Bemmann, 'The Harmony died away; The Elusive Clavichords of Gottfried Silbermann, Part II', *Clavichord International*, xix/1 (May 2015), pp.12-19 at 12. There is also an example of a pedal harpsichord used for organ practice in the mid-19th century; Peter Holman, 'The harpsichord in 19th-century Britain', *Harpsichord & Fortepiano*, xxiv/2 (Spring 2020), pp.4-14 at 6.

46 Derek Adlam, Review of 'Bach: *Preludes, Fantasies & Fugues*, Peter Sykes (clavichord)', *British Clavichord Society Newsletter*, 61 (February 2015), pp.27-30.

47 Lothar Bemmann, trans Gregory Crowell, 'Further to "The Harmony died away"; The Elusive Clavichords of Gottfried Silbermann', *Clavichord International*, xxii/2 (November 2018), pp.58-61

48 Garry Broughton, 'Bruckner's Clavichords', *British Clavichord Society Newsletter*, 65 (June 2016), pp.3-5 and 'Bruckner's Clavichords', *Bruckner Journal*, xxii/2 (July 2018), pp.17-18.

survives; he bought it in Leipzig in 1921.[49]

Remarkably, that the earliest modern reconstructions just about overlap with the last historic clavichords constructed.[50] The last of these appears to have been made in Portugal in 1858,[51] where the instrument had survived longest (it appears in customs import/export records as late as 1841), and also in Sweden.[52] In Britain, Alfred James Hipkins (1826-1903) reported in 1889 that more than one instrument was newly-made by Hoffmann of Stuttgart in 1857, 'They were made for the late Joseph Street of Lloyds'.[53] He also noted that a square piano had been converted into a clavichord in 1879 by J. G. Chatterton[54] - exactly such an instrument exists, made by Christoph Ganer in c.1786, and it may be the very 'clavichord' Hipkins mentions.[55]

Arnold Dolmetsch

As with so much in the early music revival, Dolmetsch was a key figure. Combining the qualities of a performer, teacher, instrument maker, collector

---

49   Mads Damlund and Joris Potvlieghe, 'Carl Nielsen and the Clavichord', *Clavichord International*, xix/2 (November 2015), pp.55-61; Mads Damlund, 'Carl Nielsens clavichord', *Organistbladet* (February 2016) and 'Two letters from Carl Nielsen', *Clavichord International*, xxiii/1 (May 2019), pp.17-20.

50   See for example, Eva Helenius, 'Aspects of the Clavichord in Sweden in the Nineteenth Century', in Bernard Brauchli, Alberto Galazzo and Judith Wardman (eds.), *De Clavicordio VII*, Proceedings of the International Clavichord Symposium (Magnano: Musica Antica a Magnano, 2006), pp.45–62.

51   Martin Pühringer, '"Jaras me hizo 1858" — das jüngste aller Clavichorde?', in Christian Ahrens and Gregor Klinke (eds.), *Fundament aller Clavirten Instrumenten — Das Clavichord*, 2001 Herne symposium proceedings (Munich and Salzburg, 2003), pp.155-165.

52   Gerhard Doderer and John Henry Van der Meer, *Cordofones de tecla portugueses do século XVIII: Clavicórdios, Cravos, Pianofortes e Espinetas* (Lisbon: Fundação Calouste Gulbenkian, 2005) and Gerhard Doderer, 'The Clavichord in Portugal after 1800', in Brauchli, Galazzo and Wardman (2008), pp.75-90; Eva Helenius-Öberg, *Svenskt klavikordbygge 1720-1820: studier i hantverkets teori och praktik jämte instrumentens utveckling och funktion i Sverige under klassisk tid* (Stockholm: Almqvist & Wiksell International, 1986) and Helenius (2006), pp.45-62.

53   George Grove (ed), *A dictionary of music and musicians*; Appendix, ed J. A. Fuller Maitland (London: Macmillan, 1889), p.593b.

54   A. J. Hipkins, *A Description of the History of the Pianoforte and of the Older Stringed Keyboard Instruments* (London and New York: Novello, 1896), p.64.

55   'Discovery of an "English" clavichord', *British Clavichord Society Newsletter*, 60 (October 2014), pp.38-40.

and scholar, his dynamism, self-belief and marketing skills enabled him to achieve an enormous amount, especially after his move to England in 1883, to study at the newly founded Royal College of Music. After completing his violin studies in London, his experience of instrument restoration (including a 1763 Hass by 1889) led to his first four clavichords, which used that as a model and were made in Dulwich in 1894.[56] Two others followed, made in Bloomsbury in 1895-7, and five of the six survive in Oxford, London, Edinburgh, Milan and Canada (No.4 is lost).[57] One was bought by Sir George Grove for the Royal College of Music, London, for £30. Looking back, in 1929 Dolmetsch himself described the beginnings of his clavichord making: 'In 1894 I began making clavichords, copies of a fine large instrument in my possession. The first went to Mr Fuller Maitland; Sir George Grove secured the second for the Royal College of Music; Herbert Horne decorated the third with inscriptions and paintings; it is now in a museum in Italy. The fourth is in my possession'.[58] A seventh instrument is also lost, and in 1897, with the following three (Nos.8-10), he set out in a different direction, making a group of smaller C-f^3 pentagonal instruments; Mabel Dolmetsch later described them as 'these little jewels', and spoke of 'making clavichords for musical epicures'.[59] The impact of these first instruments may have been subsequently exaggerated: already by 1898 the Royal College of Music

---

56   Lance Whitehead, 'Clavichords in Britain No.9: The 1894 Dolmetsch at the Royal College of Music', *British Clavichord Society Newsletter*, 21 (October 2001), pp.8-11.

57   See Jenny Nex and Lance Whitehead, 'The six early clavichords of Arnold Dolmetsch: their construction and inspiration', *The Galpin Society Journal*, liii (2000), pp.274-300; Peter Bavington, 'Clavichords in Britain No. 13: The Arnold Dolmetsch clavichord in St Cecilia's Hall, Edinburgh', *British Clavichord Society Newsletter*, 42 (October 2008a), pp.3-8; Carl Dolmetsch, '*Plus fait douceur que violence*: Arnold Dolmetsch and the Clavichord', *The Consort*, lii/2 (Autumn 1996), p.101; and Peter Bavington, 'Arnold Dolmetsch's clavichord making in the years before 1914', in Brauchli, Galazzo and Wardman (2008b), pp.45-58. For further background to Dolmetsch's career, see also Barnes (1995), p.235, Gregory Crowell, 'Clavichord Customers at Chickering & Sons, 1906–1914', *Clavichord International*, xvi/2 (November 2012), pp.42–46 and Palmer (1989), ch.2.

58   *Dolmetsch and his Instruments* (Haslemere: Arnold Dolmetsch, 1929), p.3.

59   Mabel Dolmetsch, *Personal Recollections of Arnold Dolmetsch* (London: Hamilton, 1957), pp.20 and 49. They are actually hexagonal, and two of the three survive, in private hands.

clavichord is described by critic John Runciman as standing 'in a kind of museum there, unplayed, untuned, unremembered'.[60]

In 1905, following bankruptcy, Dolmetsch moved to the huge piano firm of Chickering & Sons in Boston to set up an early instruments department, which made 75 instruments (34 of them clavichords) before recession put a premature end to the project.[61] The clavichords built there in 1906-10 were FF-f^3 unfretted and based on Dolmetsch's own 1784 Christian Gotthelf Hoffmann; all but five are currently accounted for, showing they have been well looked after. The purchasers were principally academics and wealthy amateurs, plus some institutions, rather than professional keyboard musicians - although the latter group did include Ferruccio Busoni, Frances Pelton Jones, Lotta Van Buren[62] and Violet Gordon Woodhouse. Dolmetsch then moved to an equivalent position with the French piano manufacturer Gaveau in Paris for three years from 1911. A small number of Gaveau clavichords survive, and the factory continued to make them after Dolmetsch departed for London in 1914. The Chickering-type model was continued, and the first of the influential small (119 cm) C-d^3 unfretted instruments appeared in 1912, made for Violet Gordon Woodhouse, who had been

---

60   Margaret Campbell, *Dolmetsch: the man and his work* (London, 1975), pp.124-125 and Joan Benson, 'The Clavichord in 20th Century America', in Maria Fernanda Cidrais Rodrigues, Manuel Morais and Rui Vieira Nery (eds.), *Livro De Homenagem a Macario Santiago Kastner* (Lisbon: Serviço de Música, 1992). In terms of actual production and availability in the post-1929 Crash era, *Fortune* magazine's August 1934 article entitled 'Clavichord Boom' seems wildly inaccurate: Palmer (1989), pp.44–45.

61   Richard Troeger, 'The Dolmetsch / Chickering Clavichords and their Model', in Brauchli, Brauchli and Galazzo (1995), pp.213-224; Gregory Crowell, 'Clavichord Customers at Chickering & Sons, 1906–1914', *Clavichord International*, xvi/2 (November 2012), pp.42-46; Peter Bavington, 'Restoration of a Chickering/Dolmetsch clavichord', *Clavichord International*, xv/2 (November 2011), pp.42-46; and Peter Bavington, *The Chickering-Dolmetsch Early-Instrument Log-Book: An Introduction*, *The Consort*, lxxix (2023), pp.61–104.

62   She spent 1922-24 at Haslemere learning clavichord building, and thereafter attempted to set up a workshop in the US; Howard Schott, 'The Clavichord Revival, 1800-1960', *Early Music*, xxxii/4 (November 2004), pp.595-603 at 599; Dalyn Cook, 'Lotta Van Buren: Pioneering Performer, Educator, and Restorer', *Clavichord International*, xxiii/1 (May 2019), pp.7-10.

playing the clavichord since 1896:[63] 'Violet's desire for a smaller instrument arose from a wish to be able to transport her clavichord to the houses of her friends, tucked away safely on a shelf, specially constructed in the front of her carriage', according to Mabel Dolmetsch. The smaller clavichords also 'were found to keep better in tune than the greater part of the longer ones and moreover, to produce a more homogenous gradation of tone colour'.[64] The lighter stringing made *bebung* easier, and they were both cheaper and also much easier to play for inexperienced pianists, which was a major selling point.

Thus, due to the vicissitudes of war and financial crisis, in the space of twenty years Dolmetsch clavichords had been made in England, the US and France, ensuring a broad geographical distribution, despite their small numbers.

After Dolmetsch

A number of makers who were trained in the Dolmetsch workshops set up in business themselves in due course;[65] one was John Challis (1907–1974), who built his first clavichord in 1926, subsequently returning to the US and becoming very interested in the use of modern materials for early keyboards. Hugh Gough (1916–1997) made his first instrument around 1935, spending his later career in America,[66] while Robert Goble (1903-1991) set up his workshop in 1937. None of these makers modelled their clavichords on originals, and in fact almost no-one did until well after the Second World War. A rare exception was Victor Hammer, who had made two large instruments in Florence in about 1929, closely based on a Joseph Luesser of c.1800 which he then owned—these were almost

---

63 Jessica Douglas-Home, *Violet: The Life and Loves of Violet Gordon Woodhouse* (London: Harvill Press, 1996); Peter Bavington, 'Clavichords in Britain 17: The Arnold Dolmetsch Clavichord at Fenton House, London', *British Clavichord Society Newsletter*, 56 (June 2013), pp.7-11 at 8; Dolmetsch (1957), p.104; the date is there given as 1913. The actual 1912 Dolmetsch/Gaveau instrument has recently been restored and has a new owner in the US as of August 2024.

64 Dolmetsch (1957), p.104.

65 See Zuckermann (1969) and John Paul, *Modern harpsichord makers* (London: Gollancz, 1981).

66 John Koster, 'Hugh Gough', *The Galpin Society Journal*, li (July 1998), pp.7-9 at 7 and John Barnes, 'Hugh Gough, 1916–1997', *British Clavichord Society Newsletter*, 8 (June 1997), p.24.

the only historical copies built between 1914 and the early 1950s.⁶⁷

Alongside these new clavichords came enthusiastic articles in the musical press such as Norman Wilkinson's 'A Note on the Clavichord and the Harpsichord' (1923): Wilkinson (1882-1934) owned a Henry Tull clavichord.⁶⁸ Pioneer performer Nellie Chaplin (1857-1930), who had come across the harpsichord in 1904 as a result of a concert invitation by Dolmetsch, bought her own 1789 Kirkman in 1908.⁶⁹ Although she does not seem to have been a clavichordist, she was aware of the instrument, and mentions Eleanor Taphouse demonstrating the 1743 Hass to John Ruskin (1819-1900) in a room over her stepfather's Oxford music shop. Thomas William Taphouse (1838-1905), a piano tuner and proprietor of his family's music business, collected numerous keyboard instruments, some of which he restored, as well as building a major historical music library, part of a collection comprising some 2,000 volumes.⁷⁰ In addition to the 1743 Hass clavichord, he owned a 1776 Nicola Palazzi, a 1784 Christian Gotthelf Hoffmann (which he later traded to Dolmetsch in exchange for an unidentified 'precious little book') and an 1803 Johann Paul Krämer & Sons.⁷¹

Another enthusiast who contributed an article to *The Musical Times* a few years later was Harold E. Watts of Enfield, who discovered the clavichord in 1936, in the hands of a university librarian friend, who had 'picked up the instrument in a neighbouring town for some 12s'; Watts wrote with great eagerness about Bach on the instrument: 'no musician really understands

---

67   See Gregory Crowell, 'Victor Hammer and the Revival of the Nineteenth-Century Clavichord', in Bernard Brauchli, Alberto Galazzo and Judith Wardman (eds.), *De Clavicordio X*, Proceedings of the International Clavichord Symposium (Magnano: Musica Antica a Magnano, 2012), pp.53–62.

68   Norman Wilkinson, 'A Note on the Clavichord and the Harpsichord', *Music and Letters*, iv/2 (April 1923), pp.162-166.

69   Nellie Chaplin, 'The Harpsichord', *Music and Letters*, iii/3 (July 1922), pp.269-273.

70   'Dotted Crotchet', 'The Musical Library of Mr. T. W. Taphouse, M. A.', *The Musical Times*, xlv/740 (1 October 1904), pp.629-636.

71   'A nineteenth-century harpsichord promoter, with a famous music collection, who had dealings with Arnold Dolmetsch', https://www.semibrevity.com.

the "48" till he has not only heard them played, but played them for himself actually on the clavichord (and harpsichord as well)'.[72]

Lambert, Goff and Tull

The impact of amateur and small-scale craft builders in the early clavichord revival should not be underestimated. For example, Herbert Lambert (1881-1936) was a professional photographer[73] who had an outsize musical influence, although his surviving instruments are very rare.[74] One example is a C-d^3 single-strung pentagonal clavichord,[75] and he also made the normal rectangular design; his goals appear to have been portability and 'a beautiful and moving quality of tone', in the words of Thomas Goff (1898-1975). In 1927 Lambert lent Herbert Howells a clavichord, which gave rise to the collection *Lambert's Clavichord*.[76] He also made an instrument for Violet Gordon Woodhouse in 1934.

Goff's own musical career (begun after eleven years as a barrister) was inspired by a meeting with Lambert in 1926, and they jointly made an instrument in 1933, listed as Goff's 'No.1'. The previous year Pamela and David McKenna had given him as a present a C-d^3 instrument made by Henry Tull, which likely encouraged Goff to start in business.[77] He was a highly successful builder, making about 125 clavichords for a very distinguished and loyal

---

[72] Harold E. Watts, 'Bach's "48": Use of the Pedal, and Other Problems', *The Musical Times*, lxxx/1160 (October 1939), pp.722-724 at 722.

[73] See for example, Herbert Lambert, *Modern British composers: seventeen portraits by Herbert Lambert* (London: F. & B. Goodwin, 1923).

[74] Lynne Mirrey, 'Pioneers of the English Clavichord Revival: 2. Herbert Lambert', *British Clavichord Society Newsletter*, 41 (June 2008), pp.8-14.

[75] Peter Bavington, 'A Clavichord by Herbert Lambert', *British Clavichord Society Newsletter*, 58 (February 2014), pp.3-6.

[76] Bruce W. Glenny, 'Herbert Howells: Aspects of Twentieth-Century English Revivalism as Seen in "Lambert's Clavichord"', in Brauchli, Brauchli and Galazzo (1995), pp.225-231.

[77] Peter Bavington, 'Henry Tull, an unsung hero of the harpsichord and clavichord revival', *Harpsichord & Fortepiano*, xxviii/2 (Spring 2024), pp.14-28.

clientele.[78] Proud of his descent from royalty, and having his own butler in his huge Pont Street house in London, it is no surprise to learn that in 1935 he made an instrument as a wedding present for the Duke of Kent.[79]

In a letter of August 1947 to John Challis, Ralph Kirkpatrick described the Goff clavichords he tried on his visit to England as 'the best' he saw: 'extremely small, too small in tone, but very fine in quality'.[80] Goff continued his standard designs - the most common of which was a C-d^3 unfretted in a beautifully veneered case - through to the 1970s, but by the time of his death (which followed close on from the retirement of his long-term cabinet-making collaborator J. C. Cobby), these designs of instrument were out of fashion with early keyboard players; Evelyn Shuckburgh and Peter Owen made a small number of clavichords of the same kind,[81] but the market had largely disappeared among performers, despite the support of composers like Haward Clarke and Stephen Dodgson.

Henry Tull (1859-1958)[82] made about 30 clavichords between about 1924 and 1941; only a few of which can now be located. Herbert Lambert owned one, as did Edith Hipkins (1854-1945), daughter of A. J. Hipkins. Tull's client list, like Goff's, included numerous eminent figures and minor aristocrats. His standard clavichord price was around £60.

---

78 Judith Wardman, 'Thomas Goff and his Clavichords: a brief introduction', *British Clavichord Society Newsletter*, 15 (October 1999), pp.18-20; Bavington (2000), pp.7-11; Richard Ireland, 'Thomas Goff Clavichord Number One Discovered', *British Clavichord Society Newsletter*, 24 (October 2002), pp.8-12; Peter Bavington, 'Tom Goff by Himself', *British Clavichord Society Newsletter*, 39 (October 2007), pp.31-32; and John Rawson, 'Thomas Goff: some memories', *British Clavichord Society Newsletter*, 40 (February 2008), pp.28-30.

79 Philip James, 'The Clavichord', *The Musical Times*, lxxvi/1106 (April 1935), pp.319-321 at 319.

80 Ralph Kirkpatrick, ed Meredith Kirkpatrick, *Letters of the American Harpsichordist and Scholar* (Rochester, NY: University of Rochester Press, 2014), p.63.

81 See James Gardner, 'Interview with Peter Owen', *The Sunday Feature* (8 May 2016).

82 Bavington (2024).

Historical models or original designs?

Arnold Dolmetsch early held that the continued copying of clavichords by Hass or Hoffman 'could only lead to stagnation and mediocrity if he did this for ever, therefore he made his own designs'; his pentagonal 'No.8' of 1897 was his first original design.[83] This belief in the possibility of improving on historical models remained the family tradition, with Carl Dolmetsch stating in 1981 that 'there is little merit in the sterile imitation in vogue today'.[84] Instrument-builder and writer John Paul noted that there was a further reason for the origin of modern engineered 'revival' designs incorporating 'improvements' for tuning stability and so on: the low pre-war price of antique instruments: 'There was little point in setting out to make a copy of a Kirkman when one could buy the real thing for £100 or so'.[85] In a letter of April 1940 to his brother, the 17-year-old collector-to-be Raymond Russell provides an explicit example: 'I may appeal to you in the course of the next few days to lend me for a while £10. I have the opportunity of buying a unique Grunnert Clavichord, carriage payed, for that sum. As a bad modern clavichord costs about £35, it might be foolish to miss the opportunity of getting a first class old instrument for £10'.[86]

Kirkpatrick and Dolmetsch

Ralph Kirkpatrick first came across the clavichord at Harvard in 1929, in the form of a five-octave Dolmetsch-Chickering of 1911.[87] His subsequent studies with Wanda Landowska were discouraging in respect of the instrument, but he was able to meet Arnold Dolmetsch in person in 1932. A visit to the Neupert collection in Nuremberg enabled him to see more

---

83   Mobbs (1996), p.12.

84   Paul (1981), p.60.

85   Paul (1981), p.261.

86   Katharine Hawnt, *'Strange Luggage': Raymond Russell, the Harpsichord and Early Music Culture in the Mid-Twentieth Century*, PhD thesis (University of Southampton, 2021), p.56. The instrument seems in fact to have been an early 20th-century small children's piano by Grunert of Johanngeorgenstadt, so not much of a bargain in the end.

87   Ralph Kirkpatrick, 'On Playing the Clavichord', *Early Music*, ix/3 (July 1981), pp.293-305 at 293. This seems to have happened in May 1932; see Kirkpatrick (2014), p.23.

historic instruments, and wrote that he was 'taken to a warehouse that was piled to the ceiling with late 18th-century clavichords. None was in playing condition, but I chose one which seemed at the time to promise well for eventual restoration and purchase. However, I have really never regretted my later decision to renounce it in favour of the small Dolmetsch clavichord which I still possess'. In retrospect this may have been something of a turning point in the early clavichord revival: had the influential figure of Kirkpatrick chosen to perform and record on the larger originals rather than the smaller modern designs, the following half-century might have been rather different. His decision was determined by his preference for J. S. over C. P. E. Bach, and by the greater portability of the four-octave instruments:

The refinements which I discovered possible on the small Dolmetsch clavichord, despite any of its inherent disadvantages, made me less and less willing to risk the unknown outcome of the restoration of the bulky five-octave old German instrument I had reserved in Nuremberg, and I cancelled that order in favour of a new Dolmetsch of my own. It was thus that my preference for the four-octave clavichord consolidated itself; it has remained constant ever since. Furthermore, it may have had an influence in the restriction of virtually all of my clavichord playing to the music playable on such an instrument, and of prime interest to me, namely that of J. S. Bach. My experiments with the genuine clavichord music of C. P. E. Bach and of other late 18th-century composers have never led me to a real desire to play this music, and it is now perfectly clear that I never will.[88]

It is not clear why the C-d^3 range was ever thought to be the 'Bach compass' (Bach actually requires GG-e^3 overall for his solo *clavier* works), but the unhistorical association of the composer with these smaller clavichords remained influential in the English-speaking world for many years, despite the fact that Carl Engel had debunked it as long ago as 1879: 'The assertion of some of our musical writers that J. S. Bach's clavichord had a compass of only four octaves is evidently unfounded'.[89] In one respect, however, the C-d^3

---

[88] Kirkpatrick (1981), p.298; this is also mentioned (August 1932) in Ralph Kirkpatrick, *Early years* (New York: Peter Lang, 1985), p.95.

[89] Carl Engel, 'Some Account of the Clavichord with Historical Notices', *The Musical Times and Singing Class Circular*, xx/439 (1 September 1879), pp.468-472 at 470.

compass was useful, in that it was so common for revival clavichords that the great majority of composers treated it as standard, thus making much of the repertoire playable on the smaller instruments.

Kirkpatrick eventually worked his way up to recording the whole *Well-Tempered Clavier* in 1959 and 1967, on instruments by Dolmetsch (1932) and Challis (1942),[90] but the experience of doing so was sufficiently traumatic that he more or less gave up the clavichord thereafter in favour of the harpsichord. Perhaps significantly, his former student Peter Wolf noted, 'Kirkpatrick, it always seemed to me, had a lifelong love-hate relationship with the instruments on which he played'.[91] Nevertheless, he also said that, 'My best recorded playing is in the second book of the "Well-Tempered Clavier," particularly in the clavichord version'.[92]

Kirkpatrick commissioned some important new works for the harpsichord, but played them relatively rarely; a 1939 solo recital exclusively of new music stands out.[93] Apparently lacking the same performing opportunities, the number of works for clavichord dedicated to him is tiny: Theodore Chanler's *Prelude and Fugue* (1934) and Gorman Hills' *Suite for Clavichord* (1947), both unpublished.

Clavichord building in Germany

As might have been expected from the land of Bach, and from one of the world centres of piano-making, Germany was not far behind England in establishing a modern clavichord tradition, but – lacking the 'Arts and Crafts' impetus – moved swiftly instead to industrial modes of production. The earliest German instrument may have been that built in 1911 by Otto Marx (1871–1964), who made a copy of the 1543 Dominicus Pisaurensis;[94]

---

90   See Knights (2020), pp.121-123. Ralph Kirkpatrick, ed. Meredith Kirkpatrick, *Reflections of an American Harpsichordist* (Rochester, NY: University of Rochester Press, 2017), ch.3.

91   Peter Wolf, 'Reminiscences of Three Performers and an Instrument Maker', *Bach*, 48/ii-49/i (2018), pp.21-43 at 41.

92   Palmer (1989).

93   Kottick (2003), p.431.

94   Bemmann (2004), p.33.

this was likely a museum-related project, producing a working copy of a valuable and delicate original. Only two years later the firm of Pfeiffer listed clavichords in their catalogue,[95] likely with the involvement of Marx. In 1926 he produced for Alfredo Cairati (1875-1960) of Stuttgart an instrument based on a large Lemme of 1787; a further one followed two years later, and this seems to have been intended for a music institution. He continued with this copying process even during the war, and in 1942 built one (possibly two) copies of the anonymous five-octave instrument in the Mozart Museum, Salzburg,[96] followed by a number of other museum copies. One other German proto-copy is an undateable but possibly very early 20th-century GG-f^3 instrument labelled 'M. J. Schamm' but probably built by Karl Maendler, and restored by Tim Hamilton some years ago.[97]

An idea of the 'factory' (rather than sole craftsman) model of harpsichord and clavichord building can be gleaned from a 1946 survey by Joseph Wörsching, which describes the pre-war industry.[98] As in the English-speaking world, the 'modernization' of the clavichord was less severe than that of the harpsichord, even though baseboard holes, laminated soundboards, heavy bridges, steel strings and weighted keys produced a touch and sonority that was unlike historic instruments; some were single-strung, and fretted instruments were very rare. Although historical single-strung clavichords are known, such as the small Stein travel clavichord of 1787, only 98 cm long,[99] the lack of resistance and low-tension stringing meant that revival clavichords of this design were hard to play in tune.

---

95   Paul Simmonds, 'The Carl A. Pfeiffer Piano Company', *Clavichord International*, xvii/1 (November 2013), pp.34-41, and 'Pfeiffer/Marx Clavichords: A Postscript', *Clavichord International*, xxii/1 (May 2018), p.24.

96   Paul Simmonds, 'What the Label does not tell us: Further Thoughts on Clavichords from the Pfeifer Workshop', in *Clavichord International*, xix/1 (May 2015), pp.20–27.

97   Tim Hamilton, 'Clavichord Labeled M. J. Schramm, München', *Tangents*, xxi (Fall 2006), pp.6-7.

98   Joseph Wörsching, *Die historic Saitenklaviere und der moderne Clavichord- und Cembalo-Bau* (Mainz: Rheingold-Verlag, 1946). Note that, with only one exception, his most recent bibliographical entries are from 1932.

99   See Rob van Acht (ed), *Harpsichords, Clavichords, Organs, Harmoniums: Checklists of the musical instrument collection of the Haags Gemeentemuseum, The Hague* (The Hague: Haags Gemeentemuseum, 1989), pp.54-55.

The pioneer German workshops included Michael and Alois Ammer (who offered an FF-f³ model),[100] Walter Merzdorf (designs of C-f³ fretted, and GG-f³),[101] J. C. Neupert (C-f³, FF-f³) and J. & P. Schiedmayer (GG-f³) – remarkably, the Schiedmayer family firm had built clavichords back in the 18th century. These makers were joined after the war by Kemper organ-builders (C-e³). Ammer's largest instrument is described as modelled on Hubert - an early example of such historic referencing, inaccurate though it may have been by modern standards, and was likely based on No.24 in the Leipzig collection. Case lengths ranged from 102-150 cm, so were never as large as the biggest historic German and Swedish instruments. Other postwar builders on the continent included Maendler, Sassmann, Sperrhake and Wittmayer, and the standard British four-octave C-d³ model was much less evident, a considerable number of makers opting for two basic sizes of clavichord determined by compass, C-f³ and FF-f³.[102] The top f³ was essential for the music of C. P. E. Bach and his contemporaries, and it is a pity that the British association of the small clavichord with J. S, Bach restricted the treble compass, and thus the instrument's ability to explore the music of the second half of the 18th century. That this repertoire has come into focus in recent decades, in concert and on record (for example, Miklós Spányi's complete C. P. E. Bach for BIS), has something to do with the availability of larger-compass instruments since.

One advantage the early German builders had was the academic research published in that language: Franz August Göhlinger wrote a doctoral thesis on the clavichord in 1910, followed by Cornelia Auerbach (the first woman to be awarded a doctorate in music in Germany), with a specialist thesis on 18th-century German clavichords. Hanns Neupert's influential short

---

100   Peter Bavington, 'Jürgen Ammer and the Ammer Dynasty', *British Clavichord Society Newsletter*, 69 (October 2017), pp.4-10. József Gát owned an Ammer (clavichords were then rare in Eastern Europe), on which he recorded some C. P. E. Bach in the early 1960s; see Brandon Bascom, *The legacy of József Gát on piano performance and Pedagogy*, DMA dissertation (University of Iowa, 2012).

101   Eckehart and Susanne Merzdorf, *Merzdorf; 100 Janhre Cembalobau* (Neulingen: J. S. Klotz, 2020).

102   Zuckermann (1969).

monograph on the instrument was published soon after WW2, but had to wait two decades for an English translation.[103]

Post-war clavichord design in Britain

In the mid-1960s, Charles Mould published a survey of historical keyboard makers in Britain,[104] and this reveals some of the emerging tendencies in clavichord building.[105]

> John Barnes: fretted C- f^3; FF- f^3 (1743 Hass copy)
> Dolmetsch: C- d^3
> Clayson & Garrett: C- d^3; FF- f^3
> John Feldberg: C- f^3; FF- f^3
> Robert Goble & Sons: AA- e^3
> Thomas Goff: four models, no details
> Alex Hodsdon: several models, no details
> John Morley: c-g^3 travel clavichord; C- d^3; GG- g^3;
>   pedal clavichord CC-g
> John Paul: C- d^3; C- f^3; FF- f^3
> Michael Thomas: 4 ½ octaves; FF- f^3
> Thomas and Rhodes: C- d^3; FF- f^3
> Dennis Woolley: C- d^3

All are described as double-strung, except those by Feldberg and the smaller Goff and Morley instruments, and having a full bottom is now fairly normal. Strikingly, only one is described as a historic copy, the Hass model of John Barnes ('If required for educational purposes this instrument can be made

---

103 Franz August Göhlinger, *Geschichte des Clavichords* (Basel: Buchdruckerei E. Birkhäuser, 1910); Cornelia Auerbach, *Die deutsche Clavichordkunst des 18.Jahrhunderts* (Kassel: Bärenreiter, 1930); Hanns Neupert, *Das Klavichord* (Kassel: Bärenreiter, 1948), trans. Ann P. P. Feldberg, *The Clavichord* (Kassel: Bärenreiter, 1965).

104 Charles Mould, 'An Index of British Makers of Historical Keyboard Instruments', *The Galpin Society Journal*, xix (April 1966), pp.101-130. Note that the appearance of a specialist model in any maker's list does not mean that it was made in any quantity, or indeed at all.

105 See also the lists in Neupert (1965), pp.63-64 and Wagner (1968, 1969).

as an exact replica of the original').[106] The Dolmetsch, Goble, Feldberg and Morley workshops employed a number of craftsmen and produced substantial numbers of early keyboards (the mid-sized Goble workshop made an impressive 750 from 1937-1981),[107] while the remaining makers were usually one or two workers producing small quantities - and almost all offered a variety of harpsichords, as well as a few spinet, virginals and ottavino designs; fortepianos were then only available from Morley.

John Sebastian Morley (1897–1988) had restored antique clavichords in the early 20th century, but 'by the early 1950's the supply of old instruments was exhausted'. Apparently using an unsigned South German unfretted C-d^3 instrument from the middle of the 18th century as a model, he created an instrument quite similar to the four-octave Dolmetsch. Production began in 1955, and by the end of the following year 30 had already been made. This was followed in 1961 by a five-octave instrument, then a pedal clavichord (1966). At their height Morley were producing 240 keyboard instruments a year,[108] and more than 2000 Morley clavichords have been made, representing more than half the firm's early keyboard output[109] - and probably more than half of all the clavichords ever made in Britain.

Under the influence of continental builders such as Rainer Schütze (1925-1989) and Martin Skowroneck (1926-2014), who were starting to make impressive historic copies in the late 1950s, the market was about to change, although perhaps more slowly for the clavichord than the harpsichord. A few years after Mould's article Wolfgang Zuckermann produced an influential survey of the trade which listed what was available worldwide;

---

106 None of the harpsichords listed are noted as historic copies, although Morley's 'Mozart piano' is described in these terms: 'The construction of this instrument is comparatively light for a piano, and it is very similar in general layout and appearance the instrument reputed to have been owned by Mozart'. For recent lists of 21st-century makers, see Bemmann (2004) and Francis Knights, 'An index of early keyboard makers', *National Early Music Association Newsletter*, vi/1 (Spring 2022), pp.126-136.

107 Paul (1981), p.101.

108 Kottick (2003), p.431.

109 Paul (1981), p.183-195; John Morley, 'Fifty Years of Clavichord Making: Robert Morley and Co.', *British Clavichord Society Newsletter*, 32 (June 2005), pp.2-5.

his acerbic comments on (in particular) the unsatisfactory design and tone of German 'factory' harpsichords proved critical in moving the market more towards historic models.[110] There are in fact a few 'revival' harpsichords and clavichords still being made around the world, but these are merely the remnants of a legacy tradition. That being said, numerous educational institutions, recording studios and the like still own (for example) Morley clavichords, so composers and players do still come across them as their first introduction to the instrument (less so the equivalent harpsichords, where the maintenance requirements are much higher, meaning that they are less likely to be retained when not in good order).

Patterns for copying

Although some museums and private individuals have allowed instrument makers generous access to disassemble and measure clavichords from their collections, many makers, as well as those from farther afield, have found it easier to use an existing technical drawing made by an expert. These became available more widely during the 1980s, and had a disproportionate influence on what models early keyboard makers offered. For example, the 1769 Taskin harpsichord and the 1763 Hass clavichord in the Russell Collection at Edinburgh - both of which are outstanding instruments - were copied by dozens of instrument makers, because accurate plans of them were easily available.[111] Both players and institutions became familiar with these and other widely copied designs, and knew what to expect from an instrument based on them. Two other factors also came into play: fashion (many amateurs observed the latest trends in instrument choices, as represented on recordings); and ease of playing by less experienced keyboardists; for example, the clavichords of Hubert score over those of Hass in the latter respect. In the mid-1990s, Koen Vermeij's survey of the most highly-regarded clavichord makers and designs of past and present showed

---

110   Zuckermann (1969). For Zuckermann's legacy, see Peter Bavington, 'Obituary: Wolfgang Joachim Zuckermann (1922–2018)', *British Clavichord Society Newsletter*, 73 (Spring 2019), pp.28-29.

111   For a list of drawings then available, see Paul (1981), pp.84-86 and, more recently, Peter Bavington, 'Technical Drawings of Clavichords', in Wardman (2005), pp.53-61.

some interesting discrepancies.[112] These choices are significant for the contemporary repertoire, as professional performances and recordings are now more likely to use historical copies than the actual revival instruments for which a great deal of the repertoire was conceived.

Kit instruments

From after the war, cost and availability problems for quality instruments led some individuals and manufacturers to provide instructions or parts for buyers to make their own, initially to designs that did not owe that much to originals. For example, in 1949, two articles in *Newnes Practical Mechanics* by J. F. Stirling explained in just a few pages how to build a C-d^3 clavichord of an allegedly historical kind,[113] while another and more technical multi-part article by J. W. Little in *Woodworker* (1964) was for a C-f^3 instrument more modern in conception. Thereafter, a number of harpsichord makers provided sets of pre-cut parts for sale as complete kit instruments, together with all the action and stringing materials. For the clavichord (unlike the harpsichord) the basic box-like construction meant that some suppliers even left buyers to source their own case wood (for example, David Bolton)[114] and thus make a further saving. The quality of the results depended on the design, materials and competence of both the manufacturer and the maker, but the best examples showed that it was in fact possible to make a successful instrument yourself.

During the 1970s and 80s kit designs gradually moved closer to historical models, and even to specialist instruments such as the triple-fretted 'King of Sweden' clavichord from Zuckermann Harpsichords in Connecticut.[115]

---

112 Koen Vermeij, 'Eighteenth-Century Lovers of the Clavichord: Which Makers did They Prefer?', in Brauchli, Brauchli and Galazzo (1995), pp.105-114.

113 Peter Bavington, 'Advice for Post-War Clavichord Constructors', *British Clavichord Society Newsletter*, 61 (February 2015), pp.41-43.

114 Christopher Stembridge, 'Obituary: David Bolton', *British Clavichord Society Newsletter*, 41 (June 2008), pp.31-32.

115 For the history of early keyboard kit instruments and their impact, see Zuckermann (1969), pp.130-135; Palmer (1989), pp.161-164; Olga Poltoratskaya, 'A guide to clavichord kits', *Tangents*, xiv (Spring 2003), pp.3-8, and Kottick (2003), p.458-465.

At present, there are a still a small number of kit suppliers still operating in the US and Europe, including the Paris Workshop, Charles Wolff, the Renaissance Workshop and Zuckermann Harpsichords, but the rise in the cost of materials means that these are a much more expensive proposition than in the past.

CHAPTER 3

PERFORMERS, CONCERTS AND RECORDINGS

As with the rising availability of clavichords during the 20th century, the increase in the number of serious performers had both a direct and indirect effect on composition – more people had a chance to hear the clavichord (playing repertoire of whatever kind), and more performers to develop an interest in new music. This often runs in parallel with the harpsichord revival, although not identical in either scope or result. From Arnold Dolmetsch's first recordings in 1931, shellac then LP vinyl discs offered an opportunity to hear an instrument anywhere a record could be played, and then – with the development of national broadcasting systems such as the BBC – those same discs, and specially recorded programmes,[116] could be heard for free. By 1935, author Philip James (a clavichord owner himself) could suggest that 'there is to-day a small but definite demand for clavichords'.[117]

Early clavichord performers

Historical concerts began as early as the 1830s, and likely originated from performer and scholar interests aroused by the early 19th century publication of music by Bach and his contemporaries; Ignaz Moscheles (1794-1870), Charles Salaman (1814-1901), Ernst Pauer (1826-1905) and others used (some) historic instruments in what were often demonstration events or lecture-recitals. The clavichord was rarely part of such events, the later-expressed view of the instrument by Rosalyn Tureck prevailing:

---

116 For example, there was a BBC broadcast called 'The Modem Clavichord' and referred to in *The Times* in March 1928; see Richard George Marshall, *The Career and reputation of Herbert Howells*, MA thesis (University of Durham, 2005), p.173. The content is unknown, but must surely have been related to the new *Lambert's Clavichord* set.

117 James (1935), p.319.

'the clavichord cannot be heard at all outside of a normal-sized room and is therefore absolutely useless in our modern concert life'.[118] However, there are examples of players and collectors showing off their instruments: James Kendrick Pyne used his original German clavichord for a recital in Manchester as early as 1885.[119]

The arrival of new instruments from the Dolmetsch workshop, together with the use of appropriately scaled venues and a growing audience for early music events, made clavichord performances somewhat more common. In 1897 Elodie Dolmetsch performed Bach's Chromatic Fantasia and Fugue on one of her husband's new Hass-model clavichords; he described it as having 'an extraordinarily powerful and beautiful tone', and the event was even mentioned in *The Times*.[120] The clavichord was also used as part of the Dolmetsch family concert tours, and the instrument 'was heard for the first time in Edinburgh' in 1897, noted a reviewer.[121] Many years later, his son Carl spoke of 'hundreds of performances in halls of many shapes and sizes'.[122]

In the US, Dolmetsch performed publicly and privately on the clavichord – including a 1908 recital at the White House for President Theodore Roosevelt, who 'seemed to enjoy the music very much',[123] while a 1909 recital at Vassar College found the audience so completely captivated 'that at the close of the performance they clubbed together and bought the instrument outright, presenting it to the college', where it remains to this day[124] (in fact, the College had bought the instrument some months previously, and

---

118 Rosalyn Tureck, 'Bach: Piano, Harpsichord or Clavichord', *American Music Teacher*, xi/3 (January-February 1962), pp.8-9, 30 at 9.

119 Holman (2020), p.9.

120 Bavington (2008b), p.3. Little is known about Elodie Lelong (Dolmetsch) (1869-c.1926), not even her death date; see Francis Knights, 'A bibliographic guide to women pioneers of the harpsichord', *Sounding Board*, xviii (April 2022), pp.73-81 at 74.

121 'Music in Edinburgh', *The Musical Times and Singing Class Circular*, xxxviii/647 (1 January 1897), p.31

122 Dolmetsch (1996).

123 'President Roosevelt Greatly Interested in Clavichord', *The Music Trades* (26 December 1908), p.9.

124 Dolmetsch (1957), p.74.

Dolmetsch was just giving the inaugural recital). His pupil Jean Stuyvesant Sinclair, who taught at Vassar from 1908, also gave concerts there on her own Dolmetsch/Chickering.[125] The performance tradition continued in the US after Dolmetsch departed, with Lotta Van Buren (1877-1960) giving clavichord recitals in New York and elsewhere from 1913 onwards, using Dolmetsch instruments.[126]

On the continent, Dorothy Swainson (1882-1959), a British but Paris-based recitalist who was a Dolmetsch pupil from 1911, began to give clavichord recitals from 1913 (she had a five-octave Dolmetsch/Gaveau instrument that she even performed on in Russia in 1914).[127] Michael Thomas later described her as 'the best clavichord player I have ever heard'.[128]

Opportunities to hear an original clavichord live remained rare, but Edgar Hunt (1906-2006) recalled a concert of Elizabethan music organized by his organist father in in Bristol in 1929, where an anonymous double-fretted instrument owned by Henry Walford Davies (and later bequeathed to Hubert Hunt) was heard: 'This clavichord was often at home on long periods of loan and was much played'.[129]

---

[125] Laurence Libin, 'Clavichords at Vassar College', *Harpsichord & Fortepiano*, xxvii/2 (Spring 2023), pp.20-25 at 21.

[126] Cook (2019). For further information about early women clavichord players, see Knights (2022) and Judith Wardman 'Women Harpsichordists and the Clavichord: some observations', *Sounding Board*, xviii (April 2022), pp.58-72.

[127] Lynne Mirrey, 'Pioneers of the English Clavichord-playing Revival: 1. Dorothy Swainson', *British Clavichord Society Newsletter*, 36 (October 2006), pp.2-6.

[128] Michael Thomas, 'The Fretted Clavichord', *The English Harpsichord Magazine*, i/2 (April 1974), pp.39-47 at 44.

[129] Edgar Hunt, 'A Harpsichord Odyssey (1)', *The English Harpsichord Magazine*, ii/8 (April 1981), pp.190-194 at 190; it is now in the Russell Collection at Edinburgh. See also Mirrey (2008), p.13.

Looking back, in 1961 Thomas Goff described Violet Gordon Woodhouse (1872-1948) as 'The most beautiful player of the clavichord',[130] and he elaborated on this at length in a 1968 radio broadcast: 'I had never heard a more wonderful and moving sound than that which her fingers drew from that frail web of golden strings'.[131] This was in 1926, and was one of the musical inspirations for Goff's eventual change of career early in the following decade.

A number of other performers were active between the wars, including Rosalyn Tureck (1913-2003), who started playing the instrument in 1929,[132] and recitalist and collector Isolde Ahlgrimm (1914-1995) in Austria.[133] Some other names have been rather forgotten, with no recordings remaining to show their skills; Joan Benson notes that 'perhaps the finest, most-forgotten clavichordist of the early twentieth century was Alfred Kreutz [1898-1960], whose sensitive playing brought listeners to tears'; but he abandoned the instrument after WW2.[134] In the US, Erwin Bodky (1896-1958) recorded some short excerpts for historical anthologies in the 1930s.

The lecture-recital

Historically-based talks formed an important part of the public's early access to live harpsichord and clavichord sound. In 1885 at the Inventions

---

130   Thomas Goff, ['Interview'], in G. A. Briggs (ed), *Audio Biographies* (Bradford: Wharfedale Wireless Works, 1961), pp.144-149 at 147.

131   Thomas Goff, 'Violet Gordon Woodhouse – Her Playing of the Clavichord', in Douglas-Home (1996), pp.320-327.

132   Rosalyn Tureck, 'Bach in the Twentieth Century', *The Musical Times*, ciii/1428 (February 1962), pp. 92-94.

133   Gregory Crowell, 'Isolde Ahlgrimm and the Historical Clavichord', *Clavichord International*, xiii/2 (November 2009), pp.58-59.

134   Joan Benson, 'Piano to Clavichord (1925-1962)', *Clavichord International*, x/2 (November 2006), pp.38-41 at 41, and 'Clavichord Technique in the mid-twentieth century', in Brauchli, Brauchli and Galazzo (1994), pp.255-257 at 256.

Exhibition,[135] and a year later for a Musical Association event in London, Alfred James Hipkins (1826-1903)[136] of Broadwoods performed Bach's Chromatic Fantasia on the 1743 Hass clavichord as part of a lecture-recital. It is worth noting that Dolmetsch had been living in London since 1883, so might even have been present on one of these occasions – and was very likely so when an earlier lecture recital took place at the Royal College of Music in November 1883, where Dolmetsch was actually studying.[137] Carl Dolmetsch noted of Hipkins that 'his delicate playing on an ancient clavichord charmed Arnold Dolmetsch'.[138] Hipkins used the same instrument in an Oxford lecture in 1890, again borrowed from its owner, Taphouse.[139] In 1885 he had given a similar lecture in London, this time using 'a good German clavichord that was once Carl Engel's, and is lent to me by Mr. Herbert Bowman'.[140] In the US, Edwin Bodky gave a lecture-recital at Harvard in April 1945, discussing three hundred years of clavichord repertoire: 'Numerous examples played on the clavichord illustrated the lecture'.[141]

Some collectors wanted their instruments used and enjoyed, and for students to be exposed to them. In 1892 Morris Steinert donated a clavichord to the Vienna Conservatory while on a visit there, 'with the proviso that the instrument should be used once a year at the public recital of the Conservatory'.[142] Another collector in Switzerland, Henry

---

135 A. J. Hipkins, 'A Lecture on Spinets, Harpsichords, and Clavichords. Read in the Music Room of the International Inventions Exhibition, October 21 and 23, 1885', *The Musical Times and Singing Class Circular*, xxvi/513 (1 November 1885), pp.646-649. Johnson (2013), p.192 lists no fewer than 17 exhibitions including historical musical instruments in Europe and North America in 1872-1904.

136 See Hipkins (1896).

137 Holman (2020), p.10.

138 Dolmetsch (1996).

139 'Mr. Hipkins's Lecture on "The Old Claviers"', *The Musical Times and Singing Class Circular*, xxxi/574 (1 December 1890), pp.719-722.

140 A. J. Hipkins, 'The Old Clavier or Keyboard Instruments; Their Use by Composers, and Technique', *Proceedings of the Musical Association*, 12th Session (1885-1886), pp.139-148.

141 Erwin Bodky, 'Clavichord Music from 1500-1800', *Bulletin of the American Musicological Society*, xi-xiii (September 1948), pp.28-29.

142 Jane Marlin, *Reminiscences of Morris Steinert* (New York: G. P. Putnam's sons, 1900), p.220.

Schumacher (1858-1923), had numerous clavichords, and there are records of them being used for performances in 1904-7.[143]

Collectors also sometimes made their instruments available to the wider public, for example, to make a point about their suitability for a particular repertoire. Carl Engel (1818-1882),[144] some of whose clavichords were evidently in working order, described the sound of one German instrument: 'Its tone, though but weak, is impressive, and really very pleasant and soothing. At any rate, it cannot but be interesting to musicians to play on the clavichord the old precious *suites* by Bach and other great masters, as they were intended to be played'.[145] In September 1879 his anonymous fretted C-g^3 instrument was placed on loan at Broadwoods in London, and he announced this in the musical press: 'I therefore invite my musical friends and my musical enemies also, if I have any - to go and examine it; or, still better, to play on it Bach's fugues precisely as he himself played them on the clavichord'.[146]

Post-war performers

The early performances were all of early music, but contemporary works began to make a appearance in concert and on record from the 1950s. Influential commercial recordings of Bach were made by Ralph Kirkpatrick (from 1949), Liselotte Selbiger (from 1952), Fritz Neumeyer (from 1955), Eta Harich-Schneider (1960), Thurston Dart (1961) and Michael Thomas (1960s, plus some important BBC broadcasts); these are the sounds that first represented the clavichord to wider audiences, using instruments by Dolmetsch, Challis, Goff, Thomas and others. Most of these players had interests in contemporary music, but only Michael Thomas recorded any on clavichord.

---

143   Harry Joelson, 'The Thirteen Clavichords of Henry Schumacher', *Clavichord International*, vii/1 (May 2003), pp.4-12.

144   See Simmonds (2008).

145   Carl Engel, *A descriptive catalogue of the music instruments in the South Kensington Museum* (London: G. E. Eyre and W. Spottiswoode, 1874), p.79.

146   Engel (1879), p.472. See also A. J. Hipkins, 'Carl Engel's Clavichords', *The Musical Times and Singing Class Circular*, xx/439 (1 September 1879), p.492.

Active performers in England after the war also included Ruth Dyson (1917-1997), an influential teacher and Howells devotee; and Valda Aveling (1920-2007) – who made few recordings, but gave some 40 clavichord recitals – and in the US from the mid-60s, Igor Kipnis (1930-2002). Susi Jeans (1911–1993), Virginia Pleasants (1911–2011) and Joan Benson (1925–2020)[147] also commissioned or performed some new music.

The contemporary clavichord truly took off at the start of the 1970s, with two key performers: Kathleen Crees (b.1944) and Annette Sachs; neither left much of a recorded legacy,[148] meaning their work has since been largely forgotten. Both also played harpsichord and piano, but the 1970s seems to have been a period of particular clavichord focus for them, which then ceased after a decade. British keyboard performer and teacher Kathleen Crees performed on clavichord in large venues such as the Purcell Room, London and Hackney Town Hall, and after emigrating to Australia gave recitals there during the late 1970s and early 80s. Between 1971 and 1975 she premiered clavichord works by William Bardwell, Haward Clarke, Malcolm Hawkins and Nigel Hildreth (then a schoolboy piano student of hers), as well as receiving a dedication from David Loeb. She also composed and performed for 'production music' recording companies like De Wolfe, writing works mostly in historical styles for clavichord, harpsichord and piano, and publishing a children's book with an LP soundtrack called *Jonathan and the Magic Clavichord* (1974).

Annette Sachs, working mostly in Belgium, was unquestionably the leading performer of avant-garde clavichord music. In 1973-1984 alone she premiered works by Luna Alcalay, Jacques Bank, Edward Boguslawski, Joanna Bruzdowicz, Joris De Laet, Yann Diederichs, Alexander Ecklebe, Karel Goeyvaerts, Fernando Grillo, Roman Haubenstock-Ramati, Piotr

---

147   See Peter Brownlee, 'Remembering Joan Benson', *Harpsichord and Fortepiano*, xxv/1 (Autumn 2020), pp.21–27.

148   See Knights (2020).

Lachert (her husband), Tera de Marez Oyens, Per Nørgård, Jorge Manuel Rosado Marques Peixinho, Godfried-Willem Raes, Jean-Louis Robert, Witold Rudziński, Bogusław Schäffer, Tomasz Sikorski, Aurel Stroë, André Van Belle and Tom Williams, as well as receiving dedications from Veit Erdmann, Lorenzo Ferrero, Marta Ptaszynska and Jadwiga Szajna-Lewandowska. It is a great pity that she made no commercial recordings of this challenging repertoire, as the broadcast excerpts that can be found on YouTube are of poor sonic quality.

Instrument owners

A number of post-war British composers have owned clavichords, such as Goff owner and former Howells pupil Haward Clarke (1904-1998), Goff owner Peter Maxwell Davies (1934-2016), and Peter Dickinson (1934-2023), who had a single-strung Hugh Gough that he performed and recorded on, and organist and teacher Alan Bullard (1947-), another Howells pupil. One of the British Clavichord Society competition prize-winners, Geoffrey Allan Taylor, bought a Dolmetsch clavichord in 1981, 'to explore the works of Byrd and Bach and many other composers each morning before breakfast',[149] but also found it a vehicle for his own music. Another composer who owned a Goff (and an Alec Hodsdon harpsichord), was Benjamin Britten, but he did not write for the instrument. Conductor Thomas Beecham had a Goff clavichord, and Prime Minister Edward Heath (1916-2005) also had and played one in No.10 Downing Street during his time in office.[150]

Recordings and Films

Clavichord recordings as a source of musical inspiration for composers seem likely to have been significant, but this is the sort of information that is rarely noted down. Recordings certainly inspired some future instrument makers, such as Hugh Gough, who in 1933 'purchased a recording of Rudolph Dolmetsch playing the harpsichord and, the next year, one of

---

149 Judith Wardman, 'Clavichord recital by Geoffrey Allan Taylor', *British Clavichord Society Newsletter*, 39 (October 2007), pp.10-11 at 10.

150 Garry Broughton, 'The Clavichord and Affairs of State (and Jazz)', *British Clavichord Society Newsletter*, 35 (June 2006), pp.21-22.

Arnold Dolmetsch playing the clavichord'.[151] One further way in which the instrument's appearance and sound were circulated was through cinema and on television; it occurs in half-a-dozen films, plus a number of documentaries; these are principally German.[152] The most important was the dramatized documentary *Chronicle of Anna Magdalena Bach* (1967), featuring Gustav Leonhardt as Bach, where the young Andreas Pangritz can be seen playing Bach's Prelude BWV 854 on a historical-model clavichord by Martin Skowroneck.

---

151 John Koster, 'Hugh Gough', *The Galpin Society Journal*, li (July 1998), pp.7-9 at 7.
152 Lothar Bemmann, 'The Clavichord in Films', in Brauchli, Galazzo and Wardman (2006), pp.249-258 at 252.

CHAPTER 4

CREATING A REPERTOIRE

The inspiration for the composition of a new work can come from many places, such as a performance, a performer, an instrument, an event or an idea, but there are several ways in which structured events or projects can give a focus, or help draw in composers who would not otherwise have thought of writing for the clavichord. These include composition competitions, publications and recording projects.

Competitions

While composition competitions for the harpsichord have an established pedigree – the Aliénor Harpsichord Composition Competition in the US has been running since 1980,[153] with the next quadrennial competition due in 2026, for example – it is only recently that the clavichord has received similar attention. Following a British Clavichord Society recital of modern music by John Cranmer and Virginia Pleasants in London in May 1997,[154] the BCS decided to hold the first ever Clavichord Composition Competition in 2004, with cash prizes from £600 to £50, thanks to a number of donors. The remit was outlined by the competition's Artistic Director Paul Simmonds in 2003: an original and unpublished solo work (in fact, a few of the pieces turned out to be repurposed from previous harpsichord or piano compositions), no longer than 8' and playable on a five-octave instrument 'by one player using only the keyboard', without electronics or amplification. A professional performance would take place in Edinburgh that August, during the BCS

---

153   See Palmer (2019), p.338 and https://hksna.org/competitions/alienor. Over 500 new scores have been generated to date.

154   See Ruby Reid Thompson, "Twentieth-Century Music for the Clavichord," *British Clavichord Society Newsletter*, 9 (October 1997): 8–9.

Clavichord Weekend there (the players were Derek Adlam, Pamela Nash, Micaela Schmitz, Joel Speerstra and Paul Simmonds – ironically, all using historical instruments from the Russell Collection).[155] An impressive forty-eight entries were received, nearly half of which came from outside the UK, and the five prize-winners were (in order) Gary Carpenter, Philippe Forget, Graham Lynch, Julia Usher and Geoffrey Alan Taylor. Simmonds estimated some 25 'worthwhile pieces' had been added to the repertoire.[156] In order to assist composers new to the instrument, practical advice about writing for the clavichord was provided, and subsequently published.[157]

In March 2007 the British Clavichord Society held a follow-up concert of modern clavichord music in London, where Julian Perkins, Micaela Schmitz and Paul Simmonds gave further performances of the prize-winning works by Carpenter and Usher, together with music by Jurg Baur, Simon Charles, Stephen Dodgson, Herbert Howells, Graham Lynch and Peter Nickol.[158]

A decade later, as part of the VII Nordic Historical Keyboard Festival held in 2018 in Kuopio, Finland, another International Clavichord Composition Competition was announced.[159] The remit was similar to the BCS event: an original, unpublished work for solo clavichord, entries anonymized, no longer than 10', prizes (€1000 and €500 respectively) for first and second, and a professional performance. The two winners were Gabriele Toia and Alissa Duryee (both clavichord performers, perhaps not coincidentally), with the other three finalists being Aspasia Naslopoulou, Timur Ismagilov and Michael Kennedy.[160]

---

155 Paul Simmonds, 'The BCS Awards for Clavichord Composition', *British Clavichord Society Newsletter*, 27 (October 2003), pp.22-23.

156 Peter Bavington, 'The British Clavichord Society Awards for Clavichord Composition, 2004', *British Clavichord Society Newsletter*, 30 (October 2004): pp.20–23.

157 Francis Knights, 'Composing for the Clavichord', in Wardman (2005), pp.9–10.

158 *British Clavichord Society Newsletter*, 37 (February 2007), p.33. The event was reviewed by Peter Bavington in the *British Clavichord Society Newsletter*, 38 (June 2007), pp.3-10.

159 http://www.nordicclavichord.org/competition2018.

160 Anna Maria McElwain, 'VII Nordic Historical Keyboard Festival', *National Early Music Association Newsletter*, ii/2 (July 2018), pp.82–86.

A further type of competition took the form of a Call for Scores at the same time over in the US, where the 'prize' was a recording on YouTube – all the pieces can still be found there.[161] In 2017 the American organist David Bohn launched the Daniel Blitz Clavichord Project,[162] the origins of which lay in a personal donation: in January 2017 Bohn was given a C-f^3 clavichord that had been made from a Zuckermann kit by his mother's cousin Daniel Blitz, who died the following March, aged 93. The Blitz project was set up in his memory, and a public call was issued for solo clavichord works (newly written, unpublished and not using electronics) consisting of 'a maximum of 100 notes'. This ingenious restriction seems to have stimulated composers world-wide, the task being so manageable, and 67 pieces were submitted, with 46 selected for recording. The variety evident is impressive, from miniaturized versions of standard forms to dances to chordal sequences to improvisatory fragments. One example is shown complete in ex.4.1, American guitarist Jay Mollerskov's *Crooked Running Water*, where individual pitches assemble into chords. The composer describes it as 'an exploration of intervallic resonance on the clavichord, inspired by the imagery of its namesake Chinese constellation'.

As part of the ongoing 'Fifteen Minutes of Fame' composition project,[163] which has so far issued more than 60 Calls for Scores involving various instruments and ensembles – each project comprises fifteen different works each of a minute's duration – a further clavichord competition took place in the US early in 2024, this time curated by keyboard player Monica Chew. In fact, two complete 'sets' were created, and the works were recorded for YouTube. While the size of works created for both these projects are small, they have between them encouraged the creation of more than a hundred new pieces for clavichord. The format is easily replicated for the future, but requires a supportive performer to lead it, and some administrative help.

---

161   https://www.youtube.com/@danielblitzclavichordproje4365.

162   Bohn has since been involved with similar length-restricted projects for organ, for toy piano and for melodica.

163   http://www.voxnovus.com/15_Minutes_of_Fame.

for the Daniel Blitz Clavichord Project
Crooked Running Water

Jay Mollerskov

Ex.4.1 Jay Mollerskov, 'Crooked Running Water' (2017), by permission of the composer

The fundamental difficulty with all competitions, successful though they are in generating new works of real quality, is that the anonymous submission method results in only the prize-winning works being recorded, published or otherwise made available – the rest of the works usually disappear, not even having been publicly listed or heard. While many submitted scores were available for inspection at the 2004 BCS Competition recital, and some have later emerged, made available elsewhere by their composers, the 'competition' format seems intrinsically problematic from this point of view.

Publications

Although there have been a small number of anthologies of music specifically aimed at clavichord players, the only attempt to include contemporary music came with a series edited by Thurston Dart for Stainer & Bell in London, where Dart was a major figure, having been involved with the Musica Britannica series for many years. 'The Little Keyboard Books' were small oblong volumes of 16 or 20 pages and priced at around 2s 6d (75 cents in the US). Dart cunningly mixed original sources with new music in the series; for example, music from a 1680s English manuscript that included two anonymous allemandes 'fitt for the Manicorde' (apparently the only such specified pieces from pre-modern Britain) appears in *Clavichord Music of the Seventeeth Century*.[164] This volume was published alongside new music by British composers, all pragmatically marketed as 'for clavichord or piano' but clearly written for the former. Dart seems to have commissioned some of the works directly, as they are dedicated to him. Despite his support of new music, he is not known to have recorded or broadcast any contemporary repertoire, even the fine 'Dart's Saraband' that Herbert Howells wrote for him in August 1956, and published in *Howells' Clavichord*.

'The Little Keyboard Books' series included Beryl Price's *Five pieces for Clavichord or Piano* (1959), Haward Clarke's *Diversions for Clavichord or Piano* (1960) and *Ten pieces* (1960), and Alan Ridout's *Suite for Clavichord (or Piano)* (1961). The *Sonatina for Clavichord or Pianoforte*, Op.18 (1964) by Alun Hoddinott was also intended for the series, having been advertised as *Three pieces* ('in preparation'), but it eventually appeared independently, due to its greater length. While the series had a short life, it was advertised regularly

---

164 Thurston Dart (ed.), *Clavichord Music of the Seventeeth Century* (London: Stainer & Bell, 1960). The manuscript was then owned by Dart, and was later published complete in Christopher Hogwood (ed.), *Fitt for the Manicorde: A seventeenth-century English collection of keyboard music* (Launton: Edition HH, 2003).

alongside other Stainer & Bell keyboard editions at the time, and the Ridout work has since been broadcast by Peter Dickinson, in 1986.[165]

Recordings

A third way that composers can be encouraged is through the offer of a recording. The first example of this was the idea of Roger Fiske at the BBC, who suggested to performer and instrument-maker Michael Thomas after a broadcast of his that new music should be written for the instrument; Thomas agreed but felt that unfamiliarity with the instrument would be a hurdle. He therefore assembled a 'loan collection' of clavichords (including the Dolmetsch/Gaveau that had belonged to the late Dorothy Swainson), and in due course works were received from Lennox Berkeley, Eugene Goossens, Anthony Scott, Robert Still and others. As well as discussing the works received for the recording in a 1961 article for *The Consort*,[166] with music examples included, he also mentioned two (now unidentified) serial pieces 'by the Liverpool composer, Thomas Wess' and a number of other works in progress. Michael Thomas had strong views on the clavichord's merits and possibilities for contemporary music, and was of the opinion that it 'should not be a backwater for precious little pieces'.

A more recent example of a recording partially populated by invited commissions is the duo disc *Chit Chat* (2023) made by Terence Charlston and Julian Perkins in 2023. This originated following the 40th anniversary of Peter Maxwell Davies' *Four Lessons for Two Keyboards*, Op.81, when Charlston wrote five new pieces of his own, adding some recent works by Alexander Blustin, Nicola LeFanu and Peter Thorne, and commissioning duos from Iain Farrington and Héloïse Werner.

---

165   Christopher Hogwood stated (private communication) that Dart's library contained copies of some unpublished contemporary works that did not make it into the published series, although none have so far been located. The extensive Dart Archive in Cambridge University Library is partially catalogued at https://archivesearch.lib.cam.ac.uk/repositories/2/resources/13435.

166   Thomas (1961); see also Thomas McGeary, 'Michael Thomas (1922–2022): an anniversary tribute', *Harpsichord & Fortepiano*, xxvii/2 (Spring 2023), pp.4-11. Most of the performer's scores from this project are in the possession of the author.

CHAPTER 5
A CENTURY OF CLAVICHORD MUSIC

Identifying the repertoire

The market for published modern clavichord music having always been small, a number of works originally written for clavichord were eventually printed with a generic 'for keyboard' designation, such as Peter Dickinson's *Five Diversions* (1963), Walter Haacke's *Ausgefallene Einfälle* (1970) and Peter Maxwell Davies' *Four Lessons for Two Keyboards* (1978). Other pieces were listed as for 'piano or clavichord', even where clearly written for the latter instrument. More recently, the ubiquity of the electronic keyboard has resulted in the return of generic assignments, sometimes with options listed as (for example) 'piano, organ, clavichord or harpsichord', as in some of the works by Timothy Broege in US. This gives the potential for broader access to players, and provided that the compass of the music fits all these instruments and the piano's sustaining pedal is not essential, does make commercial and practical sense. Prolific organist and composer Carson Cooman gives as possible instrumentation in some of his collections not only these four keyboard types, but also lute-harpsichord and harmonium. Some composers, such as Graham Lynch, have provided alternative harpsichord or clavichord versions of pieces, registration marks in the former being replaced by more detailed dynamics in the latter.

The discussion below is inevitably limited by the sheer quantity of material that needs to be covered in a limited space, the impossibility of accessing some of the scores, and the small number of sound recordings available. Within these restrictions, an attempt is made to identify the main stylistic trends, explain the origins and purposes of certain key works, and discuss the output of the most prolific clavichord composers. The organization is primarily geographical, and it has not been possible to cover every country, or every period.

Musical styles

The range of compositional styles used in clavichord music over the past century mirrors developments in classical music more widely, although neoclassicism is fairly prevalent. In terms of structures, traditional forms can be used, but are less common that might have been expected; as well as Bachian preludes & fugues, there are examples of Renaissance dances such as Pavan & Galliard, and of variation forms like the Ground (for example, the 'Plaint' from Stephen Dodgson's *Suite No.1* of 1967). Particular Baroque types of notation appear, as in the French 17th-century *Prélude non mesuré*, seen in works by David Loeb and in Matteo Messori's *A Harpsichord in the Multiverse* of 2022. The rarest mainstream style used is serialism, with Griffith Rose's *Two Humoresques* of 1958 and Donal R. Michalsky's *Fantasies* of 1961 being two examples.

The percussive element characteristic of some 20th century keyboard music (for example, the piano music of Bartók or Prokofiev) does not often appear, but Robert Moran's *Basha* (1983), for four amplified clavichords - 'amplified to an intense, aggressive volume' - according to the composer's instructions, shows that can be effective. The minimalist style (in the case of the Moran work, seventeen short sections of repeated chords in varying rhythmic and harmonic patterns overlapped to form a 'shimmering tapestry') is more recently found in parts of Muhammad-Adam Al-Sawad's *A Picture of Winter* and Aspasia Nasopoulou's *3*1 Suite*.

Jazz influence is familiar from the compositions improvised on record by Red Camp (1957) and Keith Jarrett (1986), but the best known example is from the disc of Gershwin *Porgy and Bess* arrangements made by Oscar Peterson (clavichord) and Joe Pass (guitar) in 1976.[167] Hints of jazz are

---

167   For details of these recordings, see Knights (2020). More than seventy jazz, pop, rock and folk players are listed in Knights (2020), p.236, including Tori Amos, Andrew Cronshaw, Herbie Hancock, Simon Jeffes, Booker T. Jones and Paul McCartney.

evident in Ivan Moody's *Passacaglia* (1982) and Peter Dickinson's *Suite for the centenary of Lord Berners* (1986), and while pop style (melody with arpeggiated accompaniment) is less common, it can be heard in the 2019 suite *Love, Deception, Delusion, & Counterpoint* by Michael Calabris. Many composers now work in a pragmatic polystylistic manner, and Cooman's concise and varied collection *Almanack* (2022) comprises no fewer than 76 pieces, ranging from the traditional to improvisatory fragments.

A few works use early tunings, including Douglas Leedy's *The Leaves be Green* (1975) and Jude Thomas's *Fox – Wolf – Hound* for meantone (the meantone 'wolf' dissonance explains the title of the second movement), while Alex Ness specifies 19-note equal temperament for his *Twenty chords for Daniel Blitz* of 2017.

A large number of works from 1970s and 80s Europe involve either sonic modification through amplification, or else combine clavichord with a pre-recorded tape track or electronics, for example, Hans Poort's *Berg: for clavichord and tape* (1986) and Carl Stone's *Busobong* (1980). This restricts performances to professionals and to funded events, as the tape source needs to be hired from the publisher (assuming it is even still available), or specific electronic equipment brought in and run; this is the reason why composition competitions for clavichord (see Chapter 4) make the pragmatic decision to limit works for acoustic performance only.

Clavichord music in Britain: Herbert Howells

Howells' Op.41 set *Lambert's Clavichord*, written in 1926-27, was the first published music,[168] appearing first in a limited edition copy by the Double Crown Club in 1928 then almost immediately republished by Oxford University Press in 1929. The works were written on a clavichord the composer had borrowed from Herbert Lambert,[169] and are musical portraits (together with a fugal self-portrait) of some leading figures of the day, starting

---

168 Bruce W. Glenny, 'Herbert Howells: Aspects of Twentieth-Century English Revivalism as seen in "Lambert's Clavichord"', in Brauchli, Brauchli and Galazzo (1995), pp.225-231.

169 See Mirrey (2008) and Bavington (2014).

with Lambert himself. The print run was 150 signed copies – Lambert was given copy No.1, now in the Royal College of Music library.[170] Musicians portrayed included academic Hugh Allen, scholar Edmund Fellowes, pianist Harold Samuel, and conductors Malcolm Sargent and R. R. Terry. The picturesque titles ('dream', 'toye' and so on) were derived from Elizabethan works by Farnaby and others in Fuller Maitland and Barclay Squire's edition of the Fitzwilliam Virginal Book, which had been published complete three decades earlier.[171] An early notice of *Lambert's Clavichord* (actually by one of those depicted, Hubert Foss)[172] was very positive, even including notated music examples: 'the clavichord has found its true modem exponent in the Lambert book'.[173] Foss lamented that for unfashionably traditional works of this kind, especially those from England, 'the opportunities of hearing this music have been scanty, and, curiously enough, appear to dwindle daily into silence complete ... I cannot pretend that there is much support to be found for [Howells] in his native country; worse, there is none abroad, for the walls of commercial tradition are high and seldom scaled'. The composer eventually recorded the set himself on the piano for the BBC in September 1972, aged 80,[174] but the earliest broadcast appears to be from January 1930, with three of the works arranged for cello and piano.[175]

---

170 In 1926 Lambert compiled a manuscript *Clavichord Book* (now RCM MS 8948a), including works from John Bull to Beethoven, together with Norman O'Neill's piano work *Rain on the Roof* (1919).

171 J. A. Fuller Maitland and William Barclay Squire (eds.), *The Fitzwilliam Virginal Book* (Leipzig: Breitkopf & Härtel, 1894-99).

172 Another of those portrayed also wrote about the work; H. E. Wortham, 'Lambert's Clavichord', *The Sackbut*, ix/6 (March 1929).

173 Hubert J. Foss, 'Herbert Howells: A Brief Survey of His Music', *The Musical Times*, lxxi/1044 (1 February 1930), pp.113-116.

174 Paul Spicer, *Herbert Howells* (Bridgend: Border Lines, 1998), p.177.

175 Marshall (2005), p.117.

His second collection, *Howells' Clavichord*, begun in 1941 but not completed for fifteen years, was much more substantial, difficult and advanced in style.[176] The dedicatees of the twenty pieces are a mid-century name-dropper's delight, including an impressive roster of composers (Arnold, Berkeley, Bliss, Dyson, Finzi, Hadley, Jacob, Rubbra, Walton, Vaughan Williams), performers (Boult, Bream, Dart, Malcolm) and scholars and friends of Howells. Appreciation of the collection since has been hampered by the incorrect belief that the works are more suited to the piano;[177] in fact, much of the slower music owes more to Howells' 'swell box' organ style, and everything works well on the intended instrument. The 1962 reviewer of the volume, Ivor Keys, very much appreciated the work on its own terms, even at a time when leading composers elsewhere were pushing the boundaries of atonality: 'The inhabitants of this intimate Pantheon ought to be pleased with it. Its builder is fastidious and sophisticated. His turns and returns of phrase are exactly apt to the dimensions of each piece, and even his vigour (as in 'Jacob's Brawl') is elegant ... If the Pantheon has a President it is Thomas Goff, one of whose clavichords adorns the comely publication'.

There is also a manuscript *My Lady Harewood's Pavane and Galliard* of 1949, not included in the published set; and, in a similar mode to his clavichord music, the piano sight-reading tests Howells wrote in 1924 and 1937 (published in 1993 as *Miniatures for Organ*)[178] and the *Little Book of Dances* (1928) for piano also adapt easily to the clavichord, and are recognizably related to *Lambert's Clavichord* in style.

After Howells

Haward Clarke (1904-1998) was a pupil of Herbert Howells, but one who departed from the English pastoral tradition in some interesting ways. His

---

176 Vaughan Williams wrote to Howells on 8 March 1958 on receipt of the music, saying, 'I went through the clavichord pieces, or tried to: naturally I can't play them, or always understand them so you must come and play them to me'; cited in Marshall (2005), p.102.

177 At the end of his life, the composer was on record as happy that they be played on 'any available keyboard instrument'; Palmer (2019), pp.327–328.

178 Herbert Howells, arr. Alan Ridout, *Miniatures for Organ* (Rattlesden: Kevin Mayhew, 1993).

first pieces, *Ten pieces based on Armenian Folk Songs* of 1958 and *Diversions for Clavichord or Piano* of 1960 appeared in the Stainer & Bell 'Little Keyboard Books' series in the latter year. The first set was dedicated to Thomas Goff, whose instruments Clarke used and admired. A decade later he returned to the clavichord, and Kathleen Crees became a proponent of his music, which showed a continuing interest in Armenian and Jewish melodic modality. The works are short and well designed for the instrument, with simple textured accompaniments supporting the themes; chorale-like and contrapuntal material appears from time to time. None of the later works were published and, like his equally prolific contemporary Ernst Lévy in Switzerland, he does not appear to have tried to share his music more widely.

The influence of early Howells, both in terms of English Pastoral style and the desire to create sets of short pieces, can also be seen in Peter Dyson's *Adrian's Booke* (1972), Alan Bullard's *Air and Gigue* (1974) and *Six Miniatures* (1975), and in the 21 miniatures of Trevor Hold's *The Wadenhoe Clavichord Book* (1987). While neoclassical pieces set an initial fashion for the clavichord of a slightly antiquarian musical kind, other individual post-war voices emerged, with Mátyás Seiber's *Pezzo per il clavicordo* (1951), Lennox Berkeley's *Prelude and Fugue* (1960), Alan Ridout's *Suite for Clavichord* (1961), the *Five Diversions* (1963) by Peter Dickinson, two substantial suites by Stephen Dodgson (1967, 1971) and the uncompromising *Sonatina* by Alun Hoddinott (1964) showing a variety of responses to the instrument from within the post-war English tradition. Bullard has continued writing for the instrument, with the palindromic work *Level* (2010) and a set of *Six Preludes for Clavichord* (2020).

Other British composers active since the turn of the century include Julia Usher, with *Clavicle* (2004), Peter Nickol, with collections called *Night thoughts* and *Ten miniature pieces* (2010), and Graham Lynch, who is becoming something of a specialist in writing for early keyboard instruments, thanks to the support of Finnish harpsichordist Assi Karttunen. His *Admiring Yoro Waterfall* (2001), *Petenera* (2005) and *La Forêt de Mélisande* (2023) are among the best of the 21st century clavichord repertoire.

Clavichord music in America

Despite the early presence of Dolmetsch and the manufacture of Dolmetsch/Chickering clavichords in pre-WW1 America, then the opening of the Challis workshop and the Boston early keyboard school,[179] the composing tradition there blossomed quite slowly, probably because there were not the performers to support it (the two leading American clavichordists, Ralph Kirkpatrick and Joan Benson, were away in Europe for significant periods either side of WW2). There are only a few works from before the 1960s, including pieces by Theodore Chanler (1934) and Gorman Hills (1947) for Kirkpatrick and by Griffith Rose (1958) for Benson. A chance visit to clavichord owner Robert Lagerquist in 1961 led to Donal R. Michalsky's serial *Fantasies* (1961), a challengingly modernist work only recently typeset for wider circulation.

A later composer who wrote first for Kathleen Crees then for Joan Benson was David Loeb, the largest single American contributor to the repertoire, with eleven works written over more than half a century. Over the years the style changes from metrical to free, and the influence of Japanese music becomes more apparent, especially so in *Kazejitsu* (1984) and *Yume No Kuni Sankei* (1984), where the clavichord is combined with koto and shinobue respectively. Loeb also combined the instrument with treble and bass viols in *Mists* (1969) and *Six Nocturnes* (1970) respectively – these were dedicated to Crees and to virtuoso viol player Dennis Nesbitt. This combination is not unexpected, as Loeb is also one of the leading composers of contemporary music for viol consort.

Timothy Broege, himself a clavichordist, has written seven works or collections over the past forty years, and recorded a number of them himself. These use a wide-compass instrument, and are mostly in traditional forms. Chris DeBlasio published two collections using dance forms before his early death in 1993. All these works illustrate a modern tendency for modern clavichord repertoire to use simple forms to create suite-like collections,

---

179   Kroll (2019b).

rather than more structurally-argued pieces like sonatas. Two further recent examples of this from America are Josh Schmidt's *Pieces for clavichord* (2017) and Ross James Carey's *New Year's Suite* (2019), both written for David Bohn.

Germany and Austria

The German early music revival also included a neoclassical component, where forms from the past were revisited, often using modal or broadly diatonic harmony. Examples include the work published as Piano Sonata No.1 by Ernst Pepping in 1937, *Zehn Kleine Präludien* (1945) by Kurt Hessenburg, and the 1970 *Ausgefallene Einfälle* ('Whims and Fancies') collection of 18 short pieces by Walter Haacke; all of these were published by Schott with piano mentioned first, even though the Pepping contains a note 'für mein Klavichord' and the Haacke was 'specifically designed for the clavichord's range of expressive possibilities'. They fit within the compass of the smaller instrument, and do not require sustaining pedal. Haacke published a further set with Hansen in 1985, entitled *Ein dutzend Pastorellen*. Both his collections use popular songs, chorales and some Baroque forms, give piano, harpsichord and chamber organ as performance possibilities, and are aimed at younger players. The Hessenburg set is more challenging in both technique and texture; it was written for his sister Brigette Volhard, whose husband had built her a clavichord at the end of the war.[180]

Other solo works from the post-war period include Günter Neubert's *Zwölf Stücke für clavicord* (1963), Peter Cahn's *Fünf Stücke* (1975-76), Friedrich Schenker's *Ombre de Michelangelo* (1984) and the *12 Miniaturen* (1988) by Peter Bares. None of these include a player dedication, and are mostly one-off compositions; it may be that the absence of particular performers asking for new repertoire prevented the tradition developing more widely.

In Vienna, Katharina Klement has used the clavichord extensively, in combination with other quiet instruments, with electronics, and featuring

---

180   Christine Hedinger, 'Kurt Hessenberg's "Zehn Kleine Präludien", Op.35, for Piano or Clavichord', in Bernard Brauchli, Susan Brauchli and Alberto Galazzo (eds.), *De Clavicordio III*, Proceedings of the International Clavichord Symposium (Magnano: Musica Antica a Magnano, 1997), pp.283-286.

numerous sonic special effects. She has often performed her own music, and has also recorded a number of the works.

The Low Countries

Somewhat like Britain, the musical traditions in Netherlands and in Belgium offered the same divergence between the neo-classical and the consciously modern, and the same availability of excellent instrument-makers and performers. The Netherlands tradition began with Jan van Dijk's *Partita per il clavicordio o clavicembalo* (1957), followed by Jurriaan Andriessen's *Pavane e Passamezzo* (1962) and Hendrik Andriessen's *Canzonetta* (1963), all representing more classical elements, with *Landschap* (1973) and *A la recherche d'un carillon* (1976) by Karel Goeyvaerts, *Mo-Do* (1974) by Ton de Leeuw and *Verteldgung der Wölfe* (1978) by Thom Willems representing the avant-garde – all four works are from the same decade and were performed by Annette Sachs. Most recently, Roderik de Man's *Elongated Fingers* (2017) – the title refers to the clavichord key being an extension of the player's fingers – is part of a new tradition of virtuoso works written for leading professionals, in this instance Menno van Delft.

Belgium was home to the most prolific contemporary clavichord composer, Piotr Lachert (1938–2018). Born in Poland but working in Brussels from the late 1960s, between 1972 and 1979 he created some twenty works for clavichord, nearly all premiered by Annette Sachs, his then wife. Some of these combined clavichord with tape ('bande magnetique') or slides, and, in the case of the *Concerto africain* (1978), a string orchestra (in such instances, amplification is a necessity). As with some other modern clavichord repertoire, the difficulty of accessing scores, and the lack of recordings, means that an assessment of Lachert's considerable contribution to the repertoire is not yet possible.[181]

France

Although the role of the clavichord in France in the 17th and 18th centuries

---

181   There are a number of recordings on YouTube; Sachs was the key performer of the 1970s clavichord avant-garde but made no commercial recordings of this repertoire.

has been underplayed,[182] it does seem to be the case that the strong French *clavecin* tradition both then and in the 20th century left the smaller instrument at something of a disadvantage. The presence of Dolmetsch at the Gaveau factory before WW1, and of performer Dorothy Swainson in Paris after the war, may possibly have been counteracted by the long residence of Wanda Landowska, with her known disinclination towards the instrument, a view passed on to her many students.[183] Nevertheless, there are a number of works of interest, beginning with an early *Caprice pour piano ou clavicorde* (1933), written by Robert Bernard for Marcelle de Lacour. The 21st century tradition is stronger, including Philippe Forget's *Petite Suite* of 2005 and Louis-Philippe Rivet's *Nomoi of the Great Olympian Divinities* (2006) for electro-acoustic clavichord.

Switzerland

Swiss composer and pianist Ernst Lévy (1895-1981) created over 59 short works for clavichord in a number of sets between 1956 and 1976; he began during his residence in the US and continued after his move back to Switzerland in 1966. Judging by the dedications, some were written for his pianist second wife Suzanne Levy-Loetscher (1895-1981); and several of the sets give piano as an alternative. All remained in manuscript, and there does not appear to be evidence of either recordings or performances. The style of the clavichord pieces tends to the neo-classical (he had written a theory book on tonality) and to the light-textured. Lévy was neglected in his lifetime, and did little to promote his own music ('sealing myself off from the trends of the time, I do not exist', he wrote in 1971),[184] but since his collected works have recently become available, a wider reassessment will be now possible.

---

182 Francis Knights, 'Some Observations on the Clavichord in France', *The Galpin Society Journal*, xliv (1991), pp.71-76.

183 See Francis Knights, 'Johann Sebastian Bach und das Clavichord: Argumente für ein verkanntes Instrument', *Neue Zeitschrift für Musik* (November 1990), pp.15-18.

184 Cited in Antonio Baldassarre, 'Forgotten in plain sight: Anti-Semitism, identity, and music, a portrait of Ernst Levy (1895-1981)', in Sonja Marinković, Vesna Mikić, Ivana Perković, Tijana Popović Mladjenović, Ana Stefanović and Dragana Stojanović-Novičić (eds.), *Challenges in Contemporary Musicology: Essays in Honor of Prof. Dr. Mirjana Veselinović-Hofman* (Belgrade: Faculty of Music, 2018), pp.188-244 at 224.

Jean-Jacques Dünki (1948-) is both performer and composer, and has written music for clavichord over more than 40 years, and also described the process of working with the instrument.[185] One interesting strand is his music is the tonal contrasts between different types of keyboard, as in *Tétraptéron 0-IV* (1982-92), for piano, clavichord, harpsichord and celesta. Uniquely, he has also combined clavichord with lute in *Véhicules: 8 tableaux pour lutz et clavicorde* (1998).

Scandinavia

Sweden's important role as a centre for the 18th and 19th-century clavichord meant that instruments were not difficult to find in museums and collections in modern times, but Finland now seems to be the focus for the instrument in Scandinavia, partly because of the support of institutions like the Sibelius Academy in Kuopio, and the presence of performers like Anna Maria McElwain. Nevertheless, clavichord music exists across the whole Nordic region, beginning with works by Per Nørgård and Erling Kullberg in the 1970s, but receiving special impetus in the 21st century from the Nordic Historical Keyboard Festival (2012-). Composers who have contributed to the tradition include Eero Hämeenniemi, Lauri Kilpiö, Herbert Lindholm, Mats Persson and Päivi Vartija.

Ensemble Music

Iconographical and documentary sources indicate that the clavichord was used historically in domestic ensemble music, for example to accompany a solo voice or instrument;[186] in modern times it has also been used for

---

185   See Jean-Jacques Dünki, '*Tetrapteron*, A Keyboard Quartet: The Difficulty of Integrating the Sounds of Piano, Harpsichord, Celesta and Clavichord', in Brauchli, Brauchli and Galazzo (1995), pp.249-253 and 'Composing "with" the Clavichord – A Contemporary Experience', in Brauchli, Brauchli and Galazzo (1997), pp.277-282.

186   For a catalogue of historic paintings, engravings and other clavichord representations, see Bernard Brauchli, 'A Comprehensive List of Iconographical Documents on the Clavichord', in Brauchli, Brauchli and Galazzo (1994a), pp.81–92, supplemented in successive volumes of this series; see also Bernard Brauchli, *The Clavichord* (Cambridge: Cambridge University Press, 1994b), pp.281–294.

continuo accompaniment on several recordings.[187] As well as combining the clavichord in small ensembles, such as voice and percussion in Gillian Bibby's *Musik für drei Hörer* (1971) and Denis Smalley's *Chanson de Geste* (1979),[188] contemporary composers have used it in duet with shakuhachi (Yumi Hara Cawkwell, *Nota Bene*, 2007) and with kantele (Herbert Lindholm, *Hefaistos' Dream*, 2014). The advent of amplification made possible its appearance in larger ensembles, up to orchestral size, as with Gordon Sherwood's *Concerto grosso* (1963), Jean-Louis Robert's *L'horizon des eaux* (1976), John Lambert's *Waves* (1979) and Jorge Manuel Rosado Marques Peixinho's *Mémoires-Miroirs* (1980). However, this particular phase seems to have passed, and the clavichord is again an almost exclusively acoustic instrument.

---

187   For example, by Lucy Carolan and Terence Charlston; Knights (2020).

188   For the composer's description of this work, see https://www.slideshare.net/bilsmith311/catalog-of-denis-smalley

CHAPTER 6

A GUIDE TO COMPOSING FOR THE CLAVICHORD

It used to be thought that the clavichord was too quiet to be played in public, and that the instrument should serve just for practice and private study and enjoyment, but modern experience in small halls with good acoustics has shown that it can be a successful concert instrument. In addition, it has been used in ensemble with other quiet instruments, and (using amplification) in larger groups, even to the level of concertos.

The following notes are designed to help composers become aware of some of the instrument's special qualities and limitations, and of the differences between the various types of instrument, their tone and tuning. The modern repertoire is largely divided between works written for 'revival' instruments by Dolmetsch, Goff, Goble and others, and more recent works for copies of historical clavichords. The tonal differences are considerable - a result of differences 'in the thickness of the strings and sometimes the cross-sectional area of the bridge and the weight and balance of the keys',[189] in the words of John Barnes. The music written for the very quiet, long-sustaining Goff clavichords (for example) does not transfer easily to 18th-century-type instruments. Fortunately, some (but by no means all) of the revival instruments are attractive-sounding musical instruments in their own right, meaning that there are fewer compromises needed in the name of 20th-century authenticity.

The best way of learning more is to experience the clavichord in person, and some players and makers are happy to assist composers with access to instruments; best of all is if one can be borrowed or hired, for private exploration.

---

189 Barnes (1996), p.234.

Reading and Listening

Understanding the history and design of the instrument is an essential first step, and writings by Ralph Kirkpatrick, Bernard Brauchli and Stewart Pollens are a good first step.[190] Recordings can be a mixed blessing, as they sometimes misrepresent the scale of the instrument, its volume or balance. Good recorded examples of historical and revival clavichords are however quite plentiful,[191] and a few CD recommendations below give examples of the very different sounds of fretted, unfretted and revival instruments in both historical and modern repertoire:

- *Froberger: Complete Fantasias and Canzonas* (Divine Art dda 25204, 2020), Terence Charlston, clavichord by Andreas Hermert 2009 after Anon

- *C. P. E. Bach: The Solo Keyboard Music, V* (BIS CD-964, 2000), Miklós Spányi, clavichord by Thomas Steiner 1991 after Hubert 1772

- *J. S. Bach: French Suites Nos.1-6* (Decca Eloquence 482 9398, 1961), Thurston Dart, clavichord by Thomas Goff 1950

- *Keith Jarrett: The Book of Ways* (ECM 831 396-2, 1987), Keith Jarrett, clavichords by Merzdorf

Compass, fretting and temperament

Many 20th-century clavichord works conveniently keep to the C–d^3 compass that was thought at the start of the revival to be appropriate for the majority of Bach,[192] and nearly all are for unfretted instruments (that is, where every pair of strings has its own key, rather than sharing two or three). Since the 1980s, the wider availability of historic copies—in styles dating between the 16th and 19th centuries—has led to modern works for these types of instrument,

---

190   Kirkpatrick (1981), Bernard Brauchli, *The Clavichord* (Cambridge: Cambridge University Press, 1994b), Stewart Pollens, *A history of stringed keyboard instruments* (Cambridge: Cambridge University Press, 2022).

191   Knights (2020).

192   Goff did build a C-f^3 model, and the standard Goble was AA–e^3.

especially the powerful five-octave German clavichords suitable for C. P. E. Bach, Haydn and Mozart. A small number of historic instruments (and their copies) extend by one note, to g^3, and pitches above f^3 are found in works by Timothy Broege, Ross James Carey, Philippe Forget, Terence Charlston and John Patrick Thomas; the latter two either give an alternative octave transposition or make the additional notes optional. David Loeb extends the treble further, and in *Autumn and the River* and *Fleetings* the range is FF–a^3; these were dedicated to Joan Benson, who then owned a 1780 Lindholm clavichord with such a range.[193] Generally, repertoire aimed at amateurs, or at a level of difficulty accessible by them, might do well to regard the C–d^3 unfretted clavichord as a working standard. Professionals may have access to rarer instruments, but they represent a quite small (if important) potential performing market.

Fretted clavichords offer opportunities for particular effects, as do instruments with short octaves, but need careful research as they were not standardized.[194] For example, 18th-century German double-fretted instruments had the bottom octave or so unfretted, then had two keys to a string for the higher registers, except for the notes D and A in each octave, which had their own string; however, the Iberian layout was different, with E and B having their own string instead. Fretted instruments also have a particular temperament 'built in', so the use of any other tuning system, from ¼-comma meantone to equal temperament, usually requires a major retuning or a different instrument.

Dynamics, attack and sustain

In absolute terms, relative to the modern concert grand piano, the loudest clavichords have a dynamic range of perhaps *pppp–mf*. Because the listener's and player's ears adjust quickly to the relative dynamic level, composers

---

193   Two works by Nans Bart inexplicably use notes well outside any clavichord compass, and may have been written with electronically-generated sample sounds in mind.

194   See Maria Boxall, 'The Origins and Evolution of Diatonic Fretting', *The Galpin Society Journal*, liv (May 2001), pp.143-199 and Brauchli (1994b).

have historically notated this range from about *pp–ff*. It is often rewarding to explore the dynamics at the quietest levels, although players can be reluctant to do this in concert, for fear of not being heard.

The quality of attack possible on a clavichord is very wide, from an almost imperceptible start to a note to a biting apparent *sforzando*. The upper limit is determined by the tightness of the stringing and firmness of the action, as the strings can be pushed sharp by too heavy a touch; the damper rail present on some instruments can help to prevent this. Larger, later clavichords tend to have a long sustain, due to their large soundboard; the duration can range from perhaps 2–4 seconds. The speed of decay can vary considerably, and some instruments give the illusion of a longer sustain than is actually present.

Keyboard style and texture

Although a great deal of early harpsichord, piano and organ music transfers well to the clavichord, success depends on appropriate textures. Aggressive repeated chords, dense textures and wide stretches are rarely effective, although the modern clavichord repertoire illustrates a broad variety of successful approaches, with thick or thin textures, melodic writing or counterpoint, long lines or fragmented voicing. Octaves in the bass, and sometimes even the treble, can work on the clavichord in a way that they do not on the harpsichord. In addition, dissonant chords and clusters, especially at lower volume levels, can be very effective. One of the most successful ways of writing is that common in later 18th century German keyboard music, with two-part textures dominated by a melodic right hand.

Special effects

The idea of making sounds at the clavichord not through the keyboard is by no means a new one: Friedrich Wilhelm Rust (1739-1796) wrote a Sonata in G (1792) specifically for clavichord, containing instructions as to how to create harmonics, pizzicato and tremolo effects by touching the strings and other parts of the mechanism, to create the effects of drums, muffled drums, psaltery and lute.[195]

The most detailed modern set of instructions relating to non-conventional sound production on clavichord comes in Roman Haubenstock-Ramati's *Chordophonie 2* of 1976, written for Annette Sachs. The graphic score consists of a central circle surrounded by twenty boxes containing images or drawings and a small amount of actual musical notation, to be followed in a particular order; the height of each box corresponds to the range of the instrument, and some indicated notation specifies clusters and aspects of agogics, articulation, tempo, register and ornamentation. Twenty 'actions' for sound production are indicated, which are categorized below, together with similar instructions found in works like Julia Usher's *Clavicle* (2004), Barry Guy's *Only Today* (2006) (see ex.6.1), Nissim Schaul's *Small Rooms* (2018) and Héloïse Werner's *a many-layered object* (2021). A number of works, like *Small Rooms* and Katharina Klement's *MandelMantel* (2005), are entirely comprised of such special effects.

- *Bebung* (finger vibrato) and pitch bending

- Chord clusters

- Glissando

- Pizzicato

- Tremolo

- Depressing the keys silently

- Tapping or touching the instrument (case, bottom, soundboard, bridge, tangents, listing, tuning pins, strings) with the hand, finger, fingernail, eraser, plectrum, mallet, thimble, coin, wood or glass or

---

195 See Ilton Wjuniski, 'The Twelve Sonatas by Friedrich Wilhelm Rust Published by Vincent d'Indy and their Performance on the Clavichord', in Bernard Brauchli, Alberto Galazzo and Judith Wardman (eds.), *De Clavicordio IX*, Proceedings of the International Clavichord Symposium (Magnano: Musica Antica a Magnano, 2010), pp.101–105 and Luk Vaes, 'Extraordinary Sounds and Techniques in Friedrich Wilhelm Rust's Sonata in G', *Clavichord International*, xvii/1 (May 2013), pp.14–23; these sonatas have been recorded by Ilton Wjuniski (clavichord), *Friedrich Wilhelm Rust: 12 Sonaten* (Querstand VKJK 1421, 2017).

metal rod

- String overlengths[196] – plucking, touching, brushing, strumming, stroking with a paintbrush
- Scratching or scraping the strings along their length (wound bass strings only)
- Blowing on the strings
- Paper or silk strips or other objects laid on the strings or placed between them (the 'prepared' clavichord)
- Fretting effects (more than one tangent touching the same string)

Many of these sounds are quiet, hence the amplification requested by Haubenstock-Ramati and Schaul. However, a note provided by the latter explains how this is best done: 'The purpose of the amplification is only to make audible the sounds the clavichordist is making that cannot otherwise be heard by the naked ear. It is not meant to increase the radius of the clavichord's audibility. Therefore, the volume of the loudspeaker should only be nominally higher than what the clavichord would normally produce – loud enough to richly reproduce the sounds for the audience, but no more'.[197]

---

196 For the acoustical impact of the string lengths to the right of the bridge, see Jean-Théo Jiolat, Jean-Loïc Le Carrou and Christophe d'Alessandro, 'Whistling in the Clavichord', *HAL open science*, hal-03947709v1 (2022).

197 Score instructions for Nissim Schaul, *Small Rooms, for amplified clavichord and optional Bluetooth speakers* (2018).

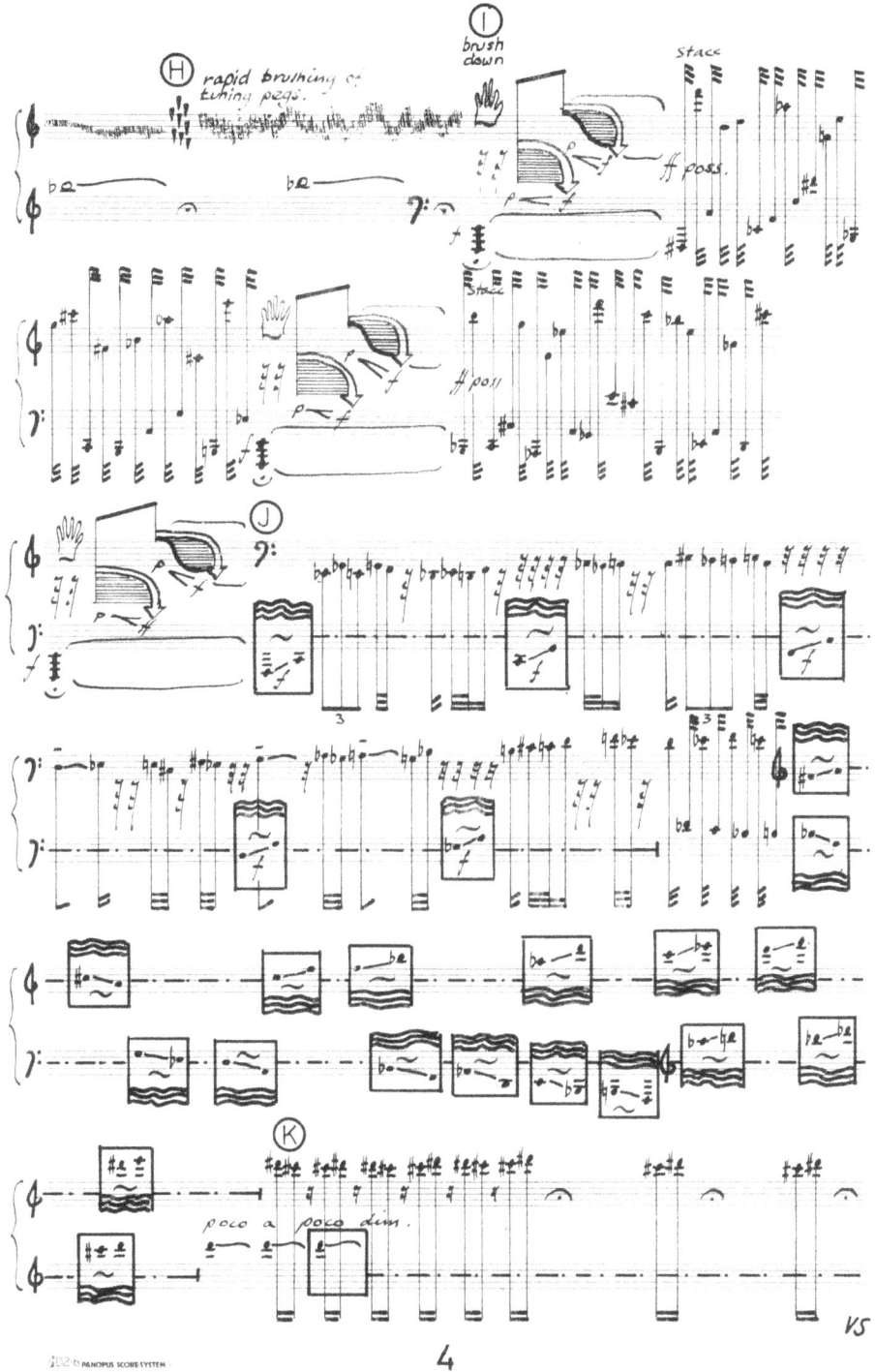

Ex.6.1 Barry Guy, 'Only Today' (2006), p.4, by permission of the composer.
Note the drawings representing the string layout

Finally, there are a number of music theatre-like works that ask the clavichordist to speak or sing, such as Tera de Marez Oyens' *And Blind She Remained* and Joanna Bruzdowicz's *Equivocitá* (both 1978), Tomasz Sikorski's *Afar a Bird* and Veit Erdmann-Abele's *Wendepunkie* (both 1981) – all performed by Annette Sachs. The seemingly obvious idea of having the player hum along to the clavichord has only been used once, in Janet Oates's *Humming Suite* (2021), which uses carefully notated vocalized humming in all four movements.

The quality of silence

Like other quiet instruments (for example, the lute) the clavichord's tone seems to emerge from silence in a way that differs from the harpsichord or piano. It is therefore worth considering carefully the purpose and meaning of rests, and of gaps between phrases – some clavichord music has a Zen-like interaction between what is heard and what is unheard. Gesture, mood and meaning, too, need to be considered within this context.

Working with performers

Unlike the harpsichord, there are very few clavichord players specializing in contemporary music, but many are happy to engage with composers, and occasionally programme 20th century or new works, which can provide contrast in a recital otherwise of early music. Professional performers will know what to expect, but students and amateurs may need more guidance as to what (if anything) they might contribute (or best be asked to contribute) during the process of a work's creation; patience is required on both sides. Some composers have very precise ideas as to how the performance should go, while others are content to let players have some input on decisions as to how a work can be effectively presented; it is best to collaborate with performers who understand their role from the very beginning, as few things are more discouraging than a composer who is disappointed by a premiere, or a performer who feels they have not lived up to a composer's imaginings.

CHAPTER 7

PERFORMING THE MODERN REPERTOIRE

Repertoire and the canon

The clavichord repertoire has not had the benefit of the equivalent harpsichord corpus, where professional performers are always on the lookout for high-quality showpieces by major composers, including concertos, and where the repertoire is supported and circulated by worklists developed for examination, audition and conservatoire purposes. A recent informal survey by Larry Palmer showed certain key works forming part of the modern harpsichord canon (including music by de Falla, Poulenc and Ligeti),[198] even if some of these works – many of which are rather difficult – are probably more admired than publicly performed.

What the contemporary clavichord repertoire offers performers is more diffuse, and relatively few works are in the repertoire of more than a handful of players, or have been recorded more than once. This is partly due to the difficulty of accessing out-of-print and manuscript music, but also because there are a relatively small number of recorded models to draw on: the complete clavichord works of Howells have only recently been recorded, and there are numerous important works yet to receive a recording – or even a second performance. The Catalogue below provides a starting point for accessing material, both in print and on disc, and the following list of 20 recommended works covering about a century of music and varying levels of difficulty is intended to draw attention to some important parts of the repertoire. This includes a number of technically challenging works (such as Gary Carpenter's *Van Assendelft's Vermeer*), and performers are reminded that

---

198   Palmer (2019), pp.339-340.

a loose sight-read through a score is not likely to give much of an impression when selecting material: it is only by actually learning a work that its qualities become evident. In addition, unfamiliar techniques (such as strumming the strings with the right hand in Alissa Duryee's *Forager's Journal*) can take a while to become natural. Those with little experience of contemporary music for early keyboards may find useful introductory material in Herbert Howells' *Lambert's Clavichord* (1928) or Carson Cooman's *Almanack: 76 Pieces for Piano or Keyboard* (2022).

Hendrik Andriessen, *'Canzonetta' voor clavichord* (1963)
Lennox Berkeley, *Prelude and Fugue* (1960)
Alan Bullard, *Level* (2018)
Gary Carpenter, *Van Assendelft's Vermeer*
Peter Dickinson, *Suite for the centenary of Lord Berners* (1986)
Stephen Dodgson, *Suite No.1 in C for Clavichord* (2008)
Alissa Duryee, *Forager's Journal* (2018)
Philippe Forget, *Petite Suite* (2005)
Barry Guy, *Only Today* (2006)
Kurt Hessenburg, *Zehn Kleine Präludien* (1945)
Alun Hoddinott, *Sonatina for Clavichord or Pianoforte* (1964)
Herbert Howells, *Lambert's Clavichord* (1928), *Howells' Clavichord* (1961)
Graham Lynch, *Petenera* (2005)
Ivan Moody, *Passacaglia* (1982)
Ernst Pepping, *Sonate 1* (1937)
Alan Ridout, *Suite for Clavichord* (1961)
Mátyás Seiber, *Pezzo per il clavicordo* (1953)
Gabriele Toia, *Tamutmutef*
Julia Usher, *Clavicle Unstrung* (2014)

Many performers turn to the clavichord in the first instance because of their interest in pre-Romantic keyboard repertoire, but there is also a question of whether players of historical instruments generally have some kind of duty or obligation to engage with the modern music written for their instrument. As composer David Loeb notes, 'The amount of eighteenth-century literature will not increase – but the contemporary repertoire will!'.[199] As the recorded representation improves, both players and audiences will be able to judge which works might best form the basis of a modern recital canon for the instrument.

Instrument choices

Significant parts of the 20th-century British clavichord repertoire were intended for Goff-type instruments; those may be unfashionably ahistorical now for Baroque music, but are still viable musical instruments in the way that the equivalent 'factory' harpsichords of the period are not. However, the older Goffs are now antiques in their own right, and quite rare and expensive, so the day may come when new copies of the best revival clavichords will need to be constructed for the sake of the modern repertoire. Pre-war Dolmetsch instruments are also increasingly expensive and hard to find, but the AA-e^3 post-war modern design made by Goble is a good substitute, and not too difficult to locate on the used market.

Programming

Choice of works for a programme will depend on elements such as performer taste, venue, acoustics, audience, recital theme and the instruments available. Even for specialist early repertoire using (for example) meantone temperament or fretting, there are modern works available which can fit such programmes. Most importantly, the clavichord should be of a suitable kind: music like Howells – written for a soft-toned instrument with a gentle attack and a significant sustain – does not always work well on historically-designed models. For mixed programmes it may be worth using more than one instrument, or else concentrating on a specialist all-20th-century programme. Even where audiences have come for earlier repertoire, a modern work can often be a successful insertion, and the theatrical gestures required by Duryee's *Forager's Journal* or Guy's *Only*

---

199   Cited in Joyce Lindorff, *Contemporary Harpsichord Music: Issues for Composers and Performers*, DMA dissertation (Juilliard School of Music, New York, 1982), p.81.

Today show an intriguingly different face of the instrument that listeners are likely to respond to. Sometimes, composer requirements are so specific that no other music can be played on that instrument, as in Rivet's *Nomoi of the Great Olympian Divinities* for electro-acoustic fretted clavichord, tuned in 'the enharmonic genus of the hypolydian mode'.

Borrowed repertoire, and arrangements

From the moment of its revival, players experimenting with this unfamiliar new instrument would have played keyboard works they already knew, and there are references to Debussy[200] and other moderns being tried out. It was Thomas Goff that suggested the Overture from Mendelssohn's *Midsummer Night's Dream* might work well on the clavichord, which is why Violet Gordon Woodhouse arranged and played it in a 1940 BBC broadcast.[201] William Walton also sent her his *Duets for Children* (1940) as possible repertoire.[202] Rex Muffat (1927-2004) made a feature of playing piano arrangements on his Goff-influenced Shuckburgh clavichord,[203] while in America Robert Haas also sought out suitable piano music for performance.[204] Composer and clavichordist Timothy Broege has recommended works by Stravinsky, Bartók, Webern and Persichetti,[205] and there are also organ manuals pieces, such as Louis Vierne's *24 Pièces en style libre*, Op.31 (1913), which can transfer effectively to the stringed instrument. As Thurston Dart pointed out many years ago, much historical (and modern) harpsichord repertoire (where not requiring two manuals or particular registrations) works very effectively on clavichord – this is still a very under-explored option.

---

200   Dorothy Swainson demonstrated Debussy preludes on clavichord; see Thomas (1961), p.97.

201   Goff (1996), p.324.

202   Garry Broughton, 'Did Picasso Play the Clavichord?', *British Clavichord Society Newsletter*, 74 (Summer 2019), pp.3-6.

203   Ian Mortimer, 'Rex Muffett (1927-2004): Teaching the clavichord', *British Clavichord Society Newsletter*, 31 (February 2005), pp.25-28.

204   Wagner (1969), pp.13-14.

205   Timothy Broege, 'What Makes It "Clavichord" (or not)?', *Tangents*, 40 (Spring 2016), p.1. See also Peter Tracton, 'Turnabout is Fair Play or Repertoire Theft for Fun and Profit', *Tangents*, xx (Spring 2006), p.5.

Working with composers

Numerous clavichord players have commissioned or performed modern works, but often only one or two pieces. The development of a repertoire for the instrument requires a longer-term relationship between performers and composers, but this is complicated by the typically non-commercial nature of the process: intrinsically small paying audience numbers by definition do not make reasonable commission fees possible; external funding is hard to get; and any performing or mechanical royalties are unlikely to amount to much.[206] Many composers appreciate this difficulty, and some are happy to provide works on the basis of (in return) two or three public performances and/or a recording. If a composer wishes to share sketches or interim versions with a player, a balance must be struck between advice from the latter about effective and viable ways of using the instrument; and a recognition that composers can have unique new perspectives, which may need a performer to acquire new technique in order to realize the music. Having received a work, it is the player's responsibility to programme it,[207] and the composer will hopefully find a performance or recording useful feedback as to the effectiveness of their music – and a stimulus to further creativity.

---

206   See https://www.prsformusic.com.
207   The author has given a number of 'inadvertent' world premieres of pieces that their dedicatee apparently never got round to performing.

CATALOGUE OF WORKS

This work-list, in composer order, of clavichord pieces includes all post-1900 pieces where the clavichord is named as the main or as an alternative keyboard instrument; a number of pieces where composers have approved performance of a piece originally for harpsichord are also included, even though this is not mentioned in the published score.

Some reference sources are very incomplete, and do not give full names or work titles; these include unidentified works by Crossley-Holland, Donati, Fujieda, Galyean, Kounadis, Oliveros, Thomas and Ward, which are not listed below. For a number of improvised, jazz-influenced or avant-garde works, no actual score exists, although there are commercial recordings. These include works by Red Camp (1957), Keith Jarrett (1987), Susan Hurley (2005), Poppy Ackroyd (2017) and Daniel Stickan (2017). Two pieces do not appear in the main sequence, as they are only known from pseudonyms provided for a competition entry: *La Belle-de-Jour* by 'Philippe Pardieu' (3', AA-f^3) and *Nine of Wands* by 'Boris Žgela' (5', FF-d#^{3}).

The format used below gives information (where known) about the composer and the work, together with performance and recording information. Instruments are given in the order specified, with '/' showing 'or', and including brackets, so 'c/(p)' is for 'clavichord (or piano)', and '2 c' is 'two clavichords'; h represents harpsichord, o is organ, p is piano, fp is fortepiano and k is keyboard, while other keyboard types are named in full. Websites are included where they are the composer or estate's own, or a substantial publisher website; and some further information can also be found in reference sources like Oxford Music Online or Wikipedia.[208] This catalogue

---

208   https://www.oxfordmusiconline.com; https://en.wikipedia.org/wiki/Main_Page.

will be updated online from time to time, like the *Clavichord Discography*.[209]

Composer (dates), website
Title (date of composition), publisher or source location and catalogue number (publication date), approximate duration in minutes, compass, instrument(s) specified, dedication, premiere, recordings, comments
Section or movement titles

CATALOGUE

Nantenaina Andriamorasata, https://www.clippings.me/vakamiarina
Notes for a peaceful world, 1', c, written for the Fifteen Minutes of Fame project, first performance by Monica Chew (2024)

Luna Alcalay (1928-2012)
Ich bin in Sehnsucht eingehüllt (1984), 40', female reciter, mezzo, c, tape, first performance by Annette Sachs and ensemble (1984), recorded on Amadeo 423 809 (1984)

Kevin Allen (1944-)
Intermezzo for clavichord, British Music Information Centre (1976), 5', c, transcription of Intermezzo for lute

Muhammad-Adam Al-Sawad (1994-)
We Grew Into Mountains, 5', C-e^{b3}, c, first performed by Anna Maria McElwain, recorded on YouTube (2017)
A Picture of Winter, 6', E-e^3, c, recorded by Anna Maria McElwain on YouTube

---

[209] See www.francisknights.co.uk.

Aaron Alter (1955-), https://aaronalter.com
Minor Mini Minuet (2017), 1', F-g^2, c, Daniel Blitz Clavichord Project, recorded by David Bohn on YouTube (2017)

Hendrik Andriessen (1892-1981)
'Canzonetta' voor clavichord, Donemus 458 (1963), 3', F-b^{b2}, c, dedicated to Caecilia Andriessen

Jurriaan Andriessen (1925-1996)
Pavane e Passamezzo per clavicembalo o clavicordio o pianoforte, Donemus (1962), 3', C-e^3, h/c/p, dedicated to Caecilia Andriessen

Louis Andriessen (1939-2021), http://www.boosey.com/composer/Louis+Andriessen
Variazioni per clavichordio, Donemus, c

Paul Angerer (1927-2017)
4 Orgelpfeifen stellen sich vor, or *4 Little Pieces for clavichord* (1946), o/c
una mesata (1985), Doblinger DB.02-00114 (1985), 11', h/o/p/c/k

Jared Isaac Aragon (1990-), https://jiaragon.weebly.com
Excessive Fragmentation (2017), 1', C#-e^3, c/h, Daniel Blitz Clavichord Project, recorded by David Bohn on YouTube (2017)

Mark Argent (1964-), http://www.markargent.com
Osterley Suite III (2004), 6', D-e^{b3}, c, first performance by Francis Knights (2006)
       Birds in the garden – Blossom – Darkening – Peaceful
A woodland walk (2008), 4', F#-d^3, c, first performance by Francis Knights (2008)

Boaz Avni, https://boazavni.musicaneo.com/about.html
A Little Prelude (1976), 1', AA-d^3, p 'or anything else you can find'

John Baboukis (1955-), https://www.aucegypt.edu/fac/johnbaboukis
Three Antiques (1975), 4', c
        Sallie – Bad News – Jhon, Come take the garbage out now
Sonata in Miniature (1977), 3', c

Nancy Bachmann, https://www.nancybachmann.com
Papillon, 1', c, written for the Fifteen Minutes of Fame project, first performance by Monica Chew (2024)

Rodrigo Baggio (1976-), http://www.rodrigobaggio.com.br
Hidden Truth (2017), 1', F-e^2, c, Daniel Blitz Clavichord Project, dedicated to David Bohn, recorded by David Bohn on YouTube (2017)

Máté Balogh (1990-), https://baloghmate.com
Peaceful Landscape with Moss, 1', c, written for the Fifteen Minutes of Fame project, dedicated to Monica Chew, first performance by Monica Chew (2024)

Jacques Bank (1943-), www.jacquesbank.net
Blue Monk (1974), Donemus (1974), 7', FF-f^3 ('octave-transpositions are allowed'), amplified c, dedicated to Annette Sachs, first performance by Annette Sachs (1974)
Thomas, Donemus (1975), 18', D-f^3, Tape and 19 instruments, including amplified c
Lied: Hommage aan Franz Schubert, Donemus (1976), 9', countertenor or mezzo, c, string quartet, percussion

William Bardwell (1915-1994)
Canzonetta Garganvilain (1971), c, first performance by Kathleen Crees (1971)

Peter Bares (1936-2014)
12 Miniaturen, Op.1655, Verlag Dohr (1988), c/p/h

Erich Barganier (1991-), http://www.barganiermusic.com
Every Pine Needle Expanded and Swelled (2017), 1', BB-e^3, c, Daniel Blitz Clavichord Project, recorded by David Bohn on YouTube (2017)

Bernard Barrell (1919-2005)
Introduction and Fugue, Op.45, Barry Brunton Music Publisher (1966), 4', C-e^3, h/c/p, dedicated to Maurice Ratliff

Joyce Barrell (1917-1989)
Two-part Inventions, Op.11, British Music Information Centre (1956), 7', c
For Maurice Ratliff (1966), British Music Information Centre (1956), 7', c

Nans Bart (1990-), http://www.pianobart.com
Notation IV, free-scores.com (2009), 2', BB-d^4 [sic] c, for David Guetta
Notation XI, free-scores.com (2009), 9', AAA-e^3 [sic], o, celesta, c, English horn

Dennis Bäsecke-Beltrametti, http://dennis-baesecke.de
Convert/to-prld&fg?, 7', D-a^2, c
    Prelude – and – Prejudice

Dennis Báthory-Kitsz (1949-), http://maltedmedia.com/people/bathory
Tangents (2007), 11', C-c^3, 2 c, dedicated to Eric Somers
Clavitas (2017), 1', d-f^3, c, Daniel Blitz Clavichord Project, recorded by David Bohn on YouTube (2017)

Patrick Bebelaar (1971-), http://www.patrickbebelaar.com
Pantheon, recorded by the Patrick Bebelaar Trio on dml-records CD 025 (2007)

Gustavo Becerra-Schmidt (1925-2010)
Fantasia para clavicordio (1992), c

John Beckwith (1927-2022)
Keyboard Practice, Canadian Music Centre (1979), 26', four players on ten keyboards, including c, first performance by William Aide, John Beckwith, Douglas Bodie and Helena Bowkun (1979)

Karol Beffa (1973-)
Sarabande et Doubles, Gerard Billaudot Editeur PR.510078430 (2014), 14', FF#-e^3, p/h/c, commissioned by the Marcelle and Robert de Lacour Foundation, first performance by Olivier Baumont (2012)

Peter Benary (1931-2015)
Three Miniatures (1962), 4', c, recorded by Franzpeter Goebels on Folkways FM 3326 (1962)

Lennox Berkeley (1903-1989), https://www.lennoxberkeley.org.uk
Prelude and Fugue, Op.55/3, Chester (1960), 4', E-e^3, recorded by Michael Thomas on Record Society RSX 16

Robert Bernard (1900-1971)
Caprice pour piano ou clavicorde (1933), p/c, for Marcelle de Lacour

Hans Georg Bertram (1936-2013), http://www.hans-georg-bertram.de
Concerto Urbinate 2 für Orgel man., Cemb, Clavi (1962), 11', o/h/c

Gillian Bibby (1945-2023)
Musik für drei Hörer (Music for Three Listeners), Internationales Musikinstitut Darmstadt (1971), 6', single-strung c, voice, percussion

Alexander J. Blustin
Idle thoughts of owls (2017), 5', BB-d^3, 2 c, also version for c (2019), recorded by Terence Charlston and Julian Perkins on Prima Facie PFCD214 (2023)
The Grand Circling of the Cat-Turkey (2019), 5', C#-d^3, c, first performance by Francis Knights (2019)
   La Gallopavo – Monsieur Donaldo – La du Christine

Edward Boguslawski (1940-2003)
4 + 1 per clavicordio (1973), 10', prepared c, dedicated to Annette Sachs, first performance by Annette Sachs (1974)

David Bohn (1965-),
    http://www.wiscomposers.org/members/bohnd.html
Fantasy: Private Music (2006), 7', C-c^3, c, version for double-fretted clavichord
Private Song (2017), 2', C-e^1, c, Daniel Blitz Clavichord Project, recorded by David Bohn on YouTube (2017)
Prelude, 1', c-e^1 c, written for the Fifteen Minutes of Fame project, first performance by Monica Chew (2024)

James Bohn, https://www.stonehill.edu/directory/james-bohn
Jojo's Paws (2017), 1', F-f^2, c, Daniel Blitz Clavichord Project, recorded by David Bohn on YouTube (2017)

Ben Brafford
Sarabande, 1', c, written for the Fifteen Minutes of Fame project, first performance by Monica Chew (2024)

Erik Branch (1966-), https://cfcomposers.org/about-us/members/erik
    branch
La Nouvelle 'Cinquante-Cinquante' (2017), 2', C-e^3, c, Daniel Blitz Clavichord Project, dedicated to David Bohn, recorded by David Bohn on YouTube (2017)

Scott Brickman (1963-), http://academic.umfk.maine.edu/scottb
Prelude (2017), 1', E^b-b^{b2}, c, Daniel Blitz Clavichord Project, recorded by David Bohn on YouTube (2017)

Meadow Bridgham, www.bridghammusic.com
Fantasietta, 1', c, written for the Fifteen Minutes of Fame project, first performance by Monica Chew (2024)

Timothy Broege (1947-), http://www.timothybroege.com
Five Sonatas, Allaire (1983), 12', BB^b-e^{b3}, h/c/k/o, Sonatas 1-2 recorded by Timothy Broege on Allaire (2015)
A Garden in Winter, Carl Fischer Pembroke Editions (1985), 13', c/h/p
Three pieces for Clavichord or Other Keyboard Instrument (1987), Woodbridge Wilson Music Publishers (2006), 11', GG-c^3, c/k, dedicated to Carl Fudge
The Sad Pavane (2002), 4', AA-g^2, recorded by Timothy Broege on Allaire (2015)
Fantasia for clavichord, 7', FF-g3, recorded by Timothy Broege on Allaire (2015)
Partita for clavichord, 15', recorded by Timothy Broege on Allaire (2015)
Paws for a moment, 3', recorded by Timothy Broege on Allaire (2015)

John Brooks
Johnny's Clavichord Tune, 1', c, written for the Fifteen Minutes of Fame project, first performance by Monica Chew (2024)

Vanessa Brown (1965-)
A Serpentine Piece (1990), 4', c, also version for h

Ferdinand Bruckmann (1930-), http://www.dohr.de/autor bruckmann.htm
Toccata (2000), Edition Dohr 20766 (2001), 4', FF-b^2, c/(p)

Joanna Bruzdowicz (1943-2021)
Equivocitá, Musical game for clavichord, Editions Choudens (1978), 8', voice, amplified c, dedicated to Annette Sachs, first performance by Annette Sachs (1978)

Thomas Buchholz (1961-)
Kammersinfonie VIII. 'Ex-sequi' (1995), 22', flute, clarinet, violin, viola, cello, percussion, h, c, first performance by Ensemble Konfrontation (1995)

Urs Bührer (1942-)
Variationen über einen Rhythmus (1972), 10', c

Alan Bullard (1947-), http://www.alanbullard.co.uk
Air and Gigue, OUP (1974), 4', D-d³, c/(p), originally part of a suite (1973)
Six Miniatures (1975), Colne Edition (1980), 15', C-d³, c/h/p
        Prelude – Air – Interlude – Sarabande – Invention – Round Dance
Prelude (1973, rev. 2019), 2', C#-c3, c/(p), originally written to precede *Air & Gigue*
Level (2018), 6', D-d³, c, originally for marimba (2010), first performance by Francis Knights (2019)
Six Preludes for Clavichord (2020), 8', C-d³, c, first performance by Francis Knights (2020)

Christopher Butterfield (1952-), https://www.uvic.ca/finearts
        music/people/director/profile/butterfield-christopher.php
Garden Truck (1989), baroque flute, baroque violin, viola da gamba, amplified c, percussion

Peter Cahn (1927-2016)
Fünf Stücke (1975-76), Edition Kemel LR186 (2005), 7', GG^b-e^{b3}, p/(c)

Michael Calabris (1984-), https://michaelcalabriscomposer.com
Love, Deception, Delusion, & Counterpoint: A Suite of Songs without Words (2019, rev. 2021), 12', C-b², first performance by Francis Knights (2021)
        Music Box – Flowers – September – Love Song – Star-Crossed

Ross James Carey (1969-), https://www.sounz.org.nz
        contributors/1111
Serene Song (2017), 3', C-d³, c, Daniel Blitz Clavichord Project, recorded by David Bohn on YouTube (2017)
New Year's Suite (2019), 8', C-g^{b3}, c, for David Bohn
        Prelude – Burlesque – Melody – Scherzo – Pause – Toccata Finale
Summer Dreaming (2023), 1', c, written for the Fifteen Minutes of Fame

project, first performance by Monica Chew (2024)

Erik Carlson, https://midnightsledding.com
For Clavichord (2017), 1', f#-f^1, c, Daniel Blitz Clavichord Project, recorded by David Bohn on YouTube (2017)

Gary Carpenter (1951-), https://www.rncm.ac.uk/people/gary carpenter
Van Assendelft's Vermeer, 4', FF-f^3, c, dedicated to Pamela Nash, first performance by Pamela Nash (2004), recorded by Pamela Nash on NMC Records D111 (2007)

Benet Casablancas Domingo (1956-), http://www.accompositors com/compositores-curriculum.php?nIdioma=ing&idComp=29
Adagi i toccata, Clivis Publicaciones (1978), 6', c, first performance by Lidia Guerberof (1978)

Yumi Hara Cawkwell, http://www.yumiharacawkwell.co.uk
Nota Bene (2007), c and shakuhachi

Utsyo Chakraborty (2001-), https://movingclassics.tv/classicpeople utsyo-chakraborty
Whimsical Dérives, 1', c, written for the Fifteen Minutes of Fame project, first performance by Monica Chew (2024)

Theodore Chanler (1902-1961)
Prelude and Fugue (1934), Library of Congress ML96.C547 no.42, 4', c/p, dedicated to Ralph Kirkpatrick

Terence Charlston, www.charlston.co.uk
Five pieces for Two Clavichords (2019), FF-g^3/FF-f^3, 15', 2 c, first performance by Terence Charlston and Julian Perkins, recorded by Terence Charlston and Julian Perkins on Prima Facie PFCD214 (2023)

Monica Chew (1977-), https://www.monicachew.com
Snow egg (2022), 1', c
Anticipation for clavichord (2024), 2', c, dedicated to E. Jean Carroll, written for the Fifteen Minutes of Fame project, first performance by Monica Chew (2024)

Haward Clarke (1904-1998)
Ten pieces based on Armenian Folk Songs (1958), Stainer & Bell 5567 (1960), 8', F-c^3, c/p, dedicated to Thomas Goff
Diversions for Clavichord or Piano, Stainer & Bell 5466 (1960), 12', A-b^2, c/p, dedicated to Marjorie Hatton
Seven pieces (1971), 7', c-d^3, c, dedicated to Kathleen Crees, first performance by Kathleen Crees (1974)
Variations on a Nursery Tune (1971), 10', C-c^3, c/p, dedicated to Kathleen Crees, first performance by Kathleen Crees (1972)
Traditional Jewish Melodies (1973), D-c^3, 12', c/p, dedicated to Bernard Herson

>Sherele – Eliyahu – Ana halach dodech – Hanava babanot – Schulf mein zuhn – Uv'yom hashabbat – Arinu malkenu – Hora Mechudashet

Melodies (1974), c, first performance by Kathleen Crees (1974)
Eight pieces based on Armenian Folk Songs (second set), 8', E^b-c^3, c/p, dedicated to Susan and Levon Chilingirian

Dominy Clements (1964-)
Catchment, Pigment, Segment for clavichord, harpsichord or fortepiano (1991), Donemus (1992), 12', c/h/fp

D. E. Cocchetti
Liber Abaci, 1', c, written for the Fifteen Minutes of Fame project, first performance by Monica Chew (2024)

James Cohn (1928-2021), https://www.jamescohnmusic.info
Sonata in E, Subito Music (1964), 14', c, originally Piano Sonata No.3

Michael Coleman
Autumn Fugue, 1', c, written for the Fifteen Minutes of Fame project, first performance by Monica Chew (2024)

Carson Cooman (1982-), https://carsoncooman.com
Ricercari for Keyboard, Op.1014 (2013), Zimbel Press 80101342 (2013), 8', C-d^3, k/o/h/c/p/lute-harpsichord/harmonium, for Kimberley Marshall, James Woodman and Peter Sykes
Toccata sequenziale sopra 'ut re mi fa' for keyboard, Op.1063, Zimbel Press 80101352 (2014), 5', C-c^3, k/h/o/c/harmonium/p, for Allan Winkler
Prelude, Fughetta, and Allegro (2014), Zimbel Press 80101353, 6', (AA^b)/C-c^3, k/p/h/o/c/lute-harpsichord/harmonium, for Steven Sorli
Three Renaissance Dances, Op.1079 (2014), Zimbel Press 80101365, 5', C-b^{b2}, k/o/h/c/p/lute-harpsichord/harmonium, for Matthew McConnell
    Pavane – Tordion – Allemande
Pastorale (E.M.M.) (2016), 3', B-a^2, k/o/p, for Rosalind Mohnsen, in memory of her mother
Sommerlicht, Op.1287 (2018), 3', E-d^3/E-a^{b2}, 2 k/h/o, for Burkhard and Petra Mohr
Ricercare and Mantra, Soundspells Productions (2021), 5', D-a^2, k/o/p/h, for Nancy, in memory of Geffin
Almanack: 76 Pieces for Piano or Keyboard, Op.1399 (2022), Zimbel Press 80101498, 90', k/p/h/o/c/harmonium
Los pequeños tigres (2022), Soundspells Productions (2022), 2', D^b-e^{b3}, k/o/p/h

Leonardo Coral (1962-), https://geelvinck.nl/kunstenaars/leonardo
    coral-componist
Aforismos (2012), 22', BB^b-e^{b3}, c, dedicated to Anna Maria McElwain
    Prólogo – Cantabile – Lluvia – Formas en el lago congelado –
    Murmullos en el bosque – Duendes – Melodia antigua –
    La eternidad frente al lago – Canto antifonal – Tapio –
    Mar mágico – Quetzalcóatl

Paul Cowell
Cuba Night (2017), 1', F-c^3, c, Daniel Blitz Clavichord Project, recorded by David Bohn on YouTube (2017)

Michael Cunningham (1937-2022)
Icon, Seesaw (1966), c, first performance by Michael Cunningham (1966), published as part of the piano collection *Portraits for Modern Dance*

Alvin Curran (1938-), http://www.alvincurran.com
Inner city #iv/1 (2003), p/(c)

Jim Dalton, https://bostonconservatory.berklee.edu/directory/jim dalton
Harmonic Labyrinth and Little Blue Bourée, 1', c, written for the Fifteen Minutes of Fame project, first performance by Monica Chew (2024)

Douglas DaSilva (1969-), http://www.burkeandbagley.com/dasilva html
Moggy Hollow Dance (2017), 1', E-d^3, c, Daniel Blitz Clavichord Project, recorded by David Bohn on YouTube (2017)

Peter Maxwell Davies (1934-2016)
Four Lessons for Two Keyboards, Op.81, Boosey & Hawkes (1978), 7', C-e^{b3}/C-e^3, 2 k, 'originally written for two clavichords', first performed Sylvia Junge and Bernard Roberts (1978), recorded by Terence Charlston and Julian Perkins on Prima Facie PFCD214 (2023)

Doug Davis
Reverie (2017), 1', g-f^3, c, Daniel Blitz Clavichord Project, recorded by David Bohn on YouTube (2017)

Chris DeBlasio (1959-1993)
Dances for Clavichord (1988), Wayne Leupold Editions WL610010 (2006), 9', AA-e^3, c, dedicated to Andrew de Masi, first performance by Andrew de

Masi (1988)
>   Vivo – Moderato Assai – Andantino – Adagio – Allegro Vivace

Three Dances for Clavichord, Logos Foundation (1986), 5', c, dedicated to Andrew de Masi (Two Dances), first performance by Andrew de Masi (1986)

Joris De Laet (1947-)
Blasphemia fatale (1977), 15', c, electronic organ, tape, dedicated to Annette Sachs, first performance by Annette Sachs and Piotr Lachert (1977)

Federico Demi (1948-)
Pearl Girl, American Music Center (1978), 99', opera including c

Philip DeWalt, http://philipdewalt.com
Toccata for Harfinger, c

Thomas Dézsy (1967-), http://www.thomasdesi.com
Die Da-Vinci-Formel (1999), 90', p, c, electronics

Peter Dickinson (1934-2023), https://peterdickinson.info
Variations on a French Folk Song (Variations on 'Sur Le Pont d'Avignon'), Novello (1957), 8', h/c
Five Diversions (1963), Novello 19558 (1966), 12', C-e^3, k, dedicated to Bridget Dickinson, recorded by Peter Dickinson on Heritage HTGCD 259 (1989)
Suite for the centenary of Lord Berners, Novello (1986), 13', BB^b-e^3, c, first performance by Peter Dickinson (1986), recorded by Peter Dickinson on Heritage HTGCD 259 (1989)
>   Blues – Jig – March – Dirge – Waltz

Yann Diederichs (1952-)
Kene (1978), 15', amplified c, dedicated to Annette Sachs, first performance by Annette Sachs (1978)
Kene 2 (1978), 9', c

Jan van Dijk (1918-2016)
Partita per il clavicordio o clavicembalo, Donemus (1957), c/h/p, dedicated to Caecilia Andriessen

Stephen Dodgson (1924-2013), http://www.stephendodgson.com
Suite No.1 in C for Clavichord (1967), Chappell 20 718 (1974) and Cadenza Music (2008), 15', C-c³, c, dedicated to Elizabeth Maconchy, first performance by Valda Aveling (1967), recorded by Julian Perkins on Campion Cameo 2088 (2009)
> Little Fanfare – First Air – Plaint – Pantomime – Greater Fanfare – Second Air – Tambourin – Last Fanfare

Suite No.2 in E♭ for Clavichord (1971), Chappell 20 717 (1974) and Cadenza Music (2008), 13', C-d³, c, dedicated to Valda Aveling, first performance by Valda Aveling (1971), recorded by Julian Perkins on Campion Cameo 2088 (2009)
> Overture – First Fanfare – A Dream – Second Fanfare – A Fancy – Round Dance

Thomas Donahue (1953-)
Soliloquy (1989), 2', h/c

David Drexler (1967-), https://drexlermusic.com
Tiny Cheesehead Toccata (2017), 1', a♭-d³, c, Daniel Blitz Clavichord Project, recorded by David Bohn on YouTube (2017)

Max Drischner (1891-1971)
Variationen über das Marienlied 'Wunderschön prächtige' (1963)

Colin Dudman
The fingers have it (2021), 2 c

Robert Duisberg (1953-)
Light and Quick (1978), 3', c, first performance by Silvia Kind (1978)

Slowly, Freely (1978), 3', c, first performance by Silvia Kind (1978)

David Duke (1950-)
7 Clavichord Pieces, Canadian Music Centre (1975), 7', c, dedicated to Melissa Hardy, first performance by David Bulmer (1976)

Jean-Jacques Dünki (1948-), https://dunki.ch/en
Abdere Kinderstücke (1960-2002), c
Tú .. no tienes imaginación, Swiss Music Service (1979), instrumental and vocal ensemble including c
Versi di Danilo Dolci, Swiss Music Service (1982), soprano and instrumental ensemble including c
Pour Valentin Claudio (1988)
Kammerstuck III auf den Namen Robert Schumann (1989)
Etudes pour le clavier (1990)
Cinq Etudes pour le clavicorde (1990-2012)
Tétraptéron 0-IV (0 1991, I/II 1982, III 1984, IV 1992), Edition Guilys SA [Tétraptéron I-II only], 14', p, c, h, celesta, recorded by Paul Clemann, Jean-Jacques Dünki, Stéphane Reymond and Pierre Subiet on Jecklin JS 289-2 (1993) and I-II only by Emmy Henz-Diémand, Jean-Jacques Dünki, Stéphane Reymond and Petra Casén on Grammont CTS-P 40-2 (1992)
Pessoa lesen (1993), 15', two voices, clarinet, cello, c
Etüde Ic (1994), 3', c
Etüde III (1996), 1', c/p
Véhicules: 8 tableaux pour lutz et clavicorde (1998), lute and c
Zwei Studien, 2', c, recorded by Jean-Jacques Dünki on Pianoversal (2018)
Andere Kinderstücke, c, for Sophia Viola, recorded by Jean-Jacques Dünki on Pianoversal (2018)

Alp Durmaz (1974-)
Meditative (2017), 2', $C-c^3$, c, Daniel Blitz Clavichord Project, recorded by David Bohn on YouTube (2017)

Alissa Duryee, https://en.alissaduryee.com
Forager's Journal (2018), 10', C-e^3, fretted c, recorded by Anna Maria McElwain on YouTube

Peter Dyson (1949-)
Adrian's Booke of Little Pieces for Children, IMSLP (1972), 17', D-b^{b2}, c, dedicated to Adrian Greeves
      Air – Frolique – Dreame – Aria – Gigue – Toccata – Chorale I – Chorale II – Courante – Bouree – Sarabande – Gavotte – Corrente – Ostinato – Siciliano – Epitaph

Wolfgang-Heinrich Ebert (1950-), http://composers21.com/compdocs/ebertwh.htm
Wasserspiele, chaconne, Op.27a (1991-92), Keturi Verlag (2005), h/c/electric p/o

Alexander Ecklebe (1904-1983)
Kleine Barocksuite (1975), 12', amplified c/h, dedicated to Annette Sachs, first performance by Annette Sachs (1975)
      Sarabande – Gavotte – Aria – Menuett – Gigue

Keith Eisenbrey (1959-)
Sonatina (1987), 8', AA-d^{b3}, c/p, IMSLP
Serenade (1988), 10', E-e^3, c/p/reed organ, IMSLP

Marios Joannou Elia (1978-), https://www.mjelia.com
Ikelos (2010), 4', c, violin, cello

Halim Abdul Messieh El-Dabb (1921-2017)
Metka' in the Art of Kita' (The Microcosm in the art of macrocosm), Logos Foundation (1961), 10', c/k
      Basseet v Samaï – Soufiane – Basseet – Samaï – Soufiane – Nawakht – Sayera

Andreas Elköf
Nodes No.1-7, recorded by Mats Persson on Compunctio CompCD008 (2013)

Kurt Ellenberger (1962-), http://www.kurtellenberger.com
Three Inventions, Assayer (2003), 7', D-eb^3, h/c/p, dedicated to Gregory Crowell

Veit Erdmann-Abele (1944-), https://www.erdmann-abele.de
Wendepunkie (1981), 11', c/p and voice (player recites), dedicated to Annette Sachs

Nicholas Fagnilli, https://fagnilliousmusic.com
Dango, 1', c, written for the Fifteen Minutes of Fame project, first performance by Monica Chew (2024)

Christian Faivre (1944-)
Petit concert pour clavicorde, freescores, 12', D-c^3, c

Iain Farrington (1977-), https://www.iainfarrington.com
Chit Chat (2020), Aria Editions (2020), 9', 2 c, recorded by Terence Charlston and Julian Perkins on Prima Facie PFCD214 (2023)
       Pep talk – Clean blues – Breezy banter

Carlotta Ferrari (1975-), http://carlottaferrari.altervista.org
Comœdia (2017), 2', C-f^3, c, IMSLP, Daniel Blitz Clavichord Project, recorded by David Bohn on YouTube (2017)
Toccata per clavicordo, IMSLP (2023), 1', AA-e^2, c, written for the Fifteen Minutes of Fame project, dedicated to Monica Chew, first performance by Monica Chew (2024)

Lorenzo Ferrero (1951-)
Ellipse II, Ricordi (1975), c (also version for h, 1976), dedicated to Annette Sachs

Michael Finnissy (1946-), http://michaelfinnissy.co.uk
White Rain (1981), p/c

Philippe Forget (1970-), https://www.philippe-forget.fr
Petite Suite, BB-f#^{3}, Hapax (2005), c, dedicated to Marcia Hadjimarkos
    Orlando's Fury – Phoebe's Tango – Frog's Intermezzo – Waltzing M

Hans Frischknecht (1939-)
6 Stücke, Swiss Music Service (1964), 9', c/p

Robert Fruehwald, https://rfruehwald.com
Silver Moon, 1', c, written for the Fifteen Minutes of Fame project, first performance by Monica Chew (2024)

Yasuharu Fukushima
Moments Musicaux, 7', E-c^3, c

James Fulkerson (1945-), http://composers21.com/compdocs
    fulkersj.htm
Now II, Media Press (1970), 18', amplified c, oscillators, trumpet, trombone, tape

Marta Gentilucci (1973-), https://martagentilucci.com
Denkwürdigkeiten aus... (2010), 7', g-c^3, speaker, violin, cello, c

John Jeffrey Gibbens (1955-), http://www.wiscomposers.org
    members/gibbens.html
Recalling Memnon (2017), 1', E-b^2, c, Daniel Blitz Clavichord Project, recorded by David Bohn on YouTube (2017)

Gerald Gifford (1949-)
Sarabande for Jeanne (2018), 1', G-f#^{2}, c/p, dedicated to Jeanne Dolmetsch

Daniel Glaus (1957-)
Trilogie III - als ein durch scheiend Glas, Swiss Music Service (1984), 15', c, alto flute, h

Laurence Glazier, www.laurenceglazier.com
Sonata for clavichord and flute (1991, rev. 2006), C-d^3, flute and c
Adagio (2000), 4', C-d^3, flute and c

Heiner Goebbels (1952-), https://www.heinergoebbels.com
Harrypatari (1995-96), Ricordi Berlin (2009), zither, marimba, cimbalom, bass guitar, c

Karel Goeyvaerts (1923-1993), https://karelgoeyvaerts.be
Landschap, Centre Belge de Documentation Musicale (1973), 8', amplified c, dedicated to Annette Sachs, first performance by Annette Sachs (1973)
A la recherche d'un carillon (1976), 14', c, p/k, two players, dedicated to Annette Sachs, first performance by Annette Sachs and Piotr Lachert (1976)

Agustín González Acilu (1929-2023),
    https://www.agustingonzalezacilu.com
Pulsiones, Editorial de Musica Española Contemporanea (1969), 4', c/h

Eugene Goossens (1893-1962)
Forlane and Toccata for Clavichord (1960), 6', C-c^3, c, dedicated to Michael Thomas, recorded by Michael Thomas on Record Society RSX 16

Ulf Grahn (1942-2023), http://www.societyofcomposers.org/members
    UlfGrahn
Canon (2017), 1', c#-c^3, c, Daniel Blitz Clavichord Project, recorded by David Bohn on YouTube (2017)

Fernando Grillo (1945-2013)
Praeludium (1981), 8', c, dedicated to Annette Sachs, first performance by Annette Sachs (1981)

Jesse Guessford, https://www.gmu.edu/profiles/jguessfo
ENVichord 2017-09-25_21:59:04 (2017), 1', C-b^{b2}, c, Daniel Blitz Clavichord Project, recorded by David Bohn on YouTube (2017)

Friedrich Gulda (1930-2000), http://www.gulda.at
6 Etüden (1974), choir, percussion, p, electric piano, c
Für Rico (1974), c
Blues for Joe Venuti (1978), p/c
Wohin denn ich (1980), alto recorder, p, c

Barry Guy (1947-), https://mayarecordings.com
Only Today (2006), 5', FF-f^3, c, dedicated to Andreas Erismann, first performance by Francis Knights (2019)

Walter Haacke (1909-2002)
Ausgefallene Einfälle, Schott ED 6096 (1970), 24', C- f^3, p/h/c/o, 'specifically designed for the clavichord's range of expressive possibilities'
        Non lehrt Noten – Miroir simple – Miroir à l'eau – Flûte de saule – Les cinq F A – Pensées – Siciliana – Musette – Correspondances – Tierce major / grand douleur – Winteraustreiben – Phrygicum super: Mein G'müt ist mir verwirret HASLERI – Modo lidico – Toccatine mixolidica – Le diable – Partita supra: Autumn comes – In diem festivum – Ciacona
Ein dutzend Pastorellen, Hansen EHF 1063 (1985), 24', C- d^3, p/h/c/o
        Auf, auf, ihr Buben – Was soll das bedeuten? – Hirtentanz – O Freude über Freude – Kommet, ihr Hirten – Still, still – Wach, Nachtigall, wach auf – In dulci jubilo – Schlaf, schlaf – Die König aus Saba – Lasst unds das Kindelein wiegen – Königsmarsch – Schum-Schey – Gross, gross

Haflidi Hallgrimsson (1941-), https://www.hallgrimsson.org.uk
Verse II, Op.4 (1975), flute, cello, percussion, amplified c, p, first performance by Thorkell Sigurbjörnsson and ensemble (1975)

Bengt Hambraeus (1928-2000)
Tetragon - Homenaje a Pablo Picasso, for four Groups of Loudspeakers (1965), 16', voice, flute, trumpet, h, c, o, percussion; tape composition

Eero Hämeenniemi (1951-)
Trastevere Variations (2002), Sulasol, 8', c/k

Walter Harburger (1887-1967)
Suite in A minor (1903-25), h/c

Oleh Harkavyy (1968-)
Chant (2017), 1', E-g#^{2}, c, Daniel Blitz Clavichord Project, recorded by David Bohn on YouTube (2017)

Roman Haubenstock-Ramati (1919-1994)
Chordophonie 2, mobile für clavichord (1976), Edition Wilhelm Hansen EHF 1009, 13', c, dedicated to Annette Sachs, first performance by Annette Sachs (1977)

Malcolm Hawkins (1944-), https://malcolmhawkins.com
Move over, Mathilda (1975), c, first performance by Kathleen Crees (1975)

John Hawksworth (1924-2009)
Fugette (1972), c, first performance by Kathleen Crees (1972)

James Heathcote, https://www.jamesheathcote.co.uk
Normil (2017), 1', D^b-f^3, c, Daniel Blitz Clavichord Project, recorded by David Bohn on YouTube (2017)

Benjamin D. Henderson
Theme and Variations, sheetmusicplus S0.262827, 3', D-d^3, k/o/h/c/harmonium

Karl Henning (1960-), http://www.pytheasmusic.org/henning.html
The Last Man to Come to the Vineyard to Work, Op.146/1 (2017), 1', C-c#^{3}, c, Daniel Blitz Clavichord Project, recorded by David Bohn on YouTube (2017)

Alex Hersom
Thom's Flowers, sheetmusicplus S0.131309, 2', g-d^2, c, chitarra battente, from the film *Supersedure* (2016)

Kurt Hessenburg (1908-1994), http://kurthessenberg.de
Zehn Kleine Präludien, Op.35 (1945), Schott ED 1403 (1949), 15', E^b-e^{b3}, p/c, dedicated to Brigette Volhard

James Hewett (1989-), https://www.koncon.nl/en/teachers/james hewitt
Preludes on the Four Elements, 6', AA-d^{b3}, recorded by Anna Maria McElwain on YouTube (2022)
    Earth – Water – Fire – Air

Nigel Hildreth (1945-)
Five Short Pieces for Clavichord (1972), 7', GG-e^{b3}, c, first performance by Kathleen Crees of three sections (1972)
    Jazzie – Resolve – Rivulet – Marionettes – La Caccia

Gorman Hills
Suite for Clavichord (1947), Kirkpatrick Archive, Yale University, 7', c
    Waltz – Jig – Sarabande – Finale

Alun Hoddinott (1929-2008)
Sonatina for Clavichord or Pianoforte, Op.18, Stainer & Bell 5600 (1964), 10', C-b^2, c/p, dedicated to Thurston Dart, recorded by Peter Dickinson on Heritage HTGCD 259 (1989)

Trevor Hold (1939-2004)
The Wadenhoe Clavichord Book (1987), 30', GG-d^3, c

    Prelude: 'Curtain-up' – Elegy on the Death of a Favourite Cat – New Wine/Old Bottle – Dragoon's March – Chimney-Sweep! – Entrance Dance for Max Wall – Pastoral I – Pastoral II – Spade Music (for the Lamport Gnome) – Minuet: 'Sur le nom de Ravel' – Gavotte: 'A Last Year's Rose': for Roger Quilter – Jig: 'Stop-Go' – Anne playing the spinet – Bagatelle – Reflections – Grandfather Asleep – A New Dance from the West Indies (1) – Popular Song – A New Dance from the West Indies (2) – The Ship's Cat – Postlude: 'Galop'

Alan Hovhaness (1911-2000), http://www.hovhaness.com
Bare November Day, Op.210 (1964), Peters 66022 (1968), 12', F-e^{b3}, h/(o)/(c)/(p), dedicated to Jan Wallgren

    Prelude – Hymn I – Hymn II – Hymn III – Hymn IV – Hymn V

Dark River and distant bell, Op.212 (1964), Peters 66024 (1968), 3', E-d^3, h/(c)/(p), dedicated to Jan Wallgren, recorded by Timothy Broege on Allaire (2015)

Herbert Howells (1892-1983)
Lambert's Clavichord, Op.41 (1926-27), Double Crown Club (1928) and OUP (1929), 28', C- d^3, c, first performance by Herbert Howells (1929), recorded by Ruth Dyson on Wealden Prestige WS 194 (1981), by Julian Perkins on Prima Facie PFCD065/66 (2017) and by Ruth Dyson on Pickwick PCD 1018 (1992)

    Lambert's Fireside – Fellowes's Delight – Hughes's Ballet – Sargent's Fantastic Sprite – Foss's Dump – My Lord Sandwich's Dreame – Samuel's Air – De la Mare's Pavane – Sir Hugh's Galliard – H. H. His Fancy – Sir Richard's Toye

My Lady Harewood's Pavane and Galliard (1949), unpublished, dedicated to Marion Stein
Howells' Clavichord, Book 1, Novello (1961), 28', C- d^3, c, dedicated to Thomas Goff, later combined into one volume, Novello 10 0228 07,

recorded by Julian Perkins on Prima Facie PFCD065/66 (2017)

    Goff's Fireside – Patrick's Siciliano – Jacob's Brawl – Dart's Saraband – Arnold's Antic – Andrew's Air – Boult's Brangill – Rubbra's Soliloquy – Newman's Flight[210] – Dyson's Delight

Howells' Clavichord, Book 2, Novello (1961), 31', C- d^3, c, dedicated to Thomas Goff, later combined into one volume, Novello 10 0228 07, recorded by Julian Perkins on Prima Facie PFCD065/66 (2017)

    Ralph's Pavane and Galliard – Finzi's Rest – Berkeley's Rest – Walton's Toye – E. B.'s Fanfarando – Ralph's Pavane – Ralph's Galliard – Finzi's Rest – Berkeley's Hunt – Malcolm's Vision – Bliss's Ballet – Julian's Dream – Jacques's Mask – Walton's Toye

Timur Ismagilov (1982-)
Fantasia for clavichord or piano, Op.43 (2018), 7', BB-d^3, c/p, recorded by Esther Yae Ji Kim on YouTube (2018)

C. L. Jancarz
Modal Melody, 1', c, written for the Fifteen Minutes of Fame project, first performance by Monica Chew (2024)

Bernhard Jestl (1960-)
Opera brevissima (1995), 16', c

Tamsin Jones, https://tamsinjones.co.uk
Praeludium in F Mixolydian, 1', c, written for the Fifteen Minutes of Fame project, first performance by Monica Chew (2024)

Jane Johnson (1923-2016)
Appalachian Excursion (1985), 4', h/c

---

210   See Lionel Pike, 'Flights of Fancy: Codes and Keys in Howells', *Tempo*, lxii/244 (April 2008), pp.11-18.

Brian Joyce
Six Sonatinas (2015), Sheet Music Plus, 35', C-e^3, p/c
   Sonatinas No.1 in C, No.2 in G, No.3 in d, No.4 in F, No.5 in a, No.6 in D

Rudolf Jungwirth (1955-)
màschere, Op.31 (1999), c

Hans Kann (1927-2005)
Sonatine für Clavichord (1966), 8', c

Shigeru Kan-no (1959-)
Miniwerk XXXXVII: 100 Notes III (2017), 1', D^b-b^2, c, Daniel Blitz Clavichord Project, recorded by David Bohn on YouTube (2017)
Sub-Mini-Werk XXXXVI for Clavichord WVE 357a, 1', c, written for the Fifteen Minutes of Fame project, first performance by Monica Chew (2024)

Dieter Kaufmann (1941-)
Boléromanique (Olympic Games for Keyboard Instruments) (1975), 10', c, tape (2-4 h)

Friedrich Keil (1957-)
Ricercare, Variationen zu 'Mille Regretz' von Josquin des Prés (1998), 8', amplified c
fantasia (2004), 8', c

Michael Kennedy
Pavin on a Colour'd Field, 5', C-a^{b2}, c, recorded by Dalyn Cook on YouTube (2018)

Lauri Kilpiö (1974-)
Poème de jeux acoustiques (2009), c

Katharina Klement (1963-), http://www.katharinaklement.com
absences, Musikverlag Alexander Mayer (2000, rev. 2012), 13', GG-g^2, unfretted prepared c and microphones, recorded by Manon Liu Winter on Kalk CD 07 (2003)
monocle (2002-2003), 43', recorder, c, electronics
wirbel, 1:2, (die) nase, gobi 1803, zersägtes grün, prozess, spalt, rotes kraut, 1:1, isabel, nicht ohne (2003), 43', tenor recorder, bass recorder, c, melodica, electronics, monochord
soundog 1-5 (2004-2006), percussion, p, c, cello, electronics
Santa Fe, Yokohama, Sydney, Kapstadt, Ulan Bator, Zagreb (2003), 40', flute, p, c
MandelMantel (2005), 17', F-e^1, unfretted prepared c and electronics, first performance by Katharina Klement (2005)
in a mad mood, madam (2006), 10', E-e^2, unfretted prepared c and electronics, first performance by Katharina Klement (2006), recorded by Katharina Klement on Edition Zeitton ORF CD 3027 (2008)
los autodisparadores (2007), 15', recorder, p, c, electronics
project FROTH (Future Archeologies of Love and Power) (2010), 10', c and tape

Katharina Klement and **Josef Novotny**
klement/novotny 1-8 (1998), 18', zither, p, c, electronics

Francis Knights (1963-), www.francisknights.co.uk
Miniature Prelude & Fugue (2017), 1', F#-e^2, c, Daniel Blitz Clavichord Project, recorded by David Bohn on YouTube (2017)

Alfred Knüsel (1941-)
Land am Rand (1998), 4', c/h/p/celesta and percussion

Michael Kosch (1959-)
A Semblance of Memling, 1', c, written for the Fifteen Minutes of Fame project, first performance by Monica Chew (2024)

Andrew Kosinksi, https://www.andrewkosinski.com

Prisms, 2', recorded by Timothy Broege on Allaire (2016)

Johannes Kotschy (1949-)

Finisterre, Op.21, Eigenverlag (1986), 65', reciters, flute, bassoon, vibraphone, marimba, c, double bass, tape

Eberhard Kraus (1931-2003)

Variationen einer 12-Ton-Folge Girolamo Frescobaldis: Eine Toccata (1983), o/h/c

Erling Kullberg (1945-)

Turn für klavikord, cembalo eller klaver (1973), c/h/p

Jouni Kuronen (1958-)

Six Affects, Op.56, Teosto, 8', BB-d#^{3}, c

Osvaldo Lacerda (1927-2011)

Sonata (1977), 10', c/h/p

Piotr Lachert (1938-2018), http://www.lachertfoundation.eu

Il pianto, Centre Belge de Documentation Musicale (1972), 2 c, dedicated to Paolo Bortuluzzi, first performance by Annette Sachs (1973)

Utwor Na Klawikord + Klawikord (1972), 7', dedicated to Annette Sachs

Piece pour clavicorde et bande magnetique No.1, Centre Belge de Documentation Musicale (1972, revised 1973), 8', c and tape, dedicated to Annette Sachs, first performance by Annette Sachs (1972, 1974)

Piece pour clavicorde et bande magnetique No.3, Centre Belge de Documentation Musicale (1973), 9', c and tape, first performance by Annette Sachs (1973)

Piece pour clavicorde et bande magnetique No.7, Centre Belge de Documentation Musicale (1973), c and tape, first performance by Annette Sachs (1979)

Piece pour clavicorde et bande magnetique No.9, Centre Belge de Documentation Musicale (1973), c and tape, first performance by Annette Sachs (1974)

Première suite pour clavicorde, Centre Belge de Documentation Musicale (1973), c and tape, dedicated to Hans-Georg Sachs, first performance by Piotr Lachert (1974), clavichord pieces nos.4-6

Deuxième suite pour clavicorde, Centre Belge de Documentation Musicale (1973), 25', c, first performance by Annette Sachs (1973), clavichord pieces nos.11-16

Troisième Suite, 'russe', Centre Belge de Documentation Musicale (1973), 16', c, dedicated to Annette Sachs, first performance by Annette Sachs (1973)

Piece No.2, Centre Belge de Documentation Musicale (1973), 7', c and o, dedicated to Annette Sachs, first performance by Annette Sachs (1972)

Piece pour clavicorde No.8, Centre Belge de Documentation Musicale (1973), 6', c

Piece pour clavicorde No.10, Centre Belge de Documentation Musicale (1973), 3', c

Piece pour clavicorde No.17, Centre Belge de Documentation Musicale (1973), 8', c, dedicated to Britta and Klaus Sachs

De peccatis mundi, Centre Belge de Documentation Musicale (1974), 7', c, dedicated to Jacques Michiels, clavichord piece no.19

Kalejdscop, Centre Belge de Documentation Musicale (1974), 8', c, dedicated to Annette Sachs, first performance by Annette Sachs (1974), clavichord piece no.18, with slides

Relabis, Centre Belge de Documentation Musicale (1975), 3', c, first performance by Annette Sachs and Piotr Lachert (1975)

Concerto africain, Centre Belge de Documentation Musicale (1978, rev. c.2017), 23', c/p and strings, dedicated to Annette Sachs, first performance by Annette Sachs (1978)

Erotic Music (1978), 12', c, vx, actions, first performance by Annette Sachs (1978)

Le coucou, Centre Belge de Documentation Musicale (1978), 19', c and o, dedicated to Annette Sachs, first performance by Annette Sachs and Piotr Lachert (1978)

B. W. [Bob Wilson], Centre Belge de Documentation Musicale (1979), 145', c, voice, tape, dedicated to Annette Sachs, first performance by Annette

Sachs (1980)
Cadenza (Concerto Africain) (1984), 5', c

John Lambert (1926-1995)
Waves, British Music Information Centre, unpublished (1979), 25', instrumental ensemble (flute, alto flute, piccolo, oboe, english horn, alto saxophone, clarinet, bass clarinet, horn, bassoon, trombone, violin, viola, cello, double bass, vibraphone, guitar, harpsichord, tapes, synthesizer, speakers), c

Liz Lane, https://www.lizlane.co.uk
Diamond Fantasia (2019), 5', D-c^3, ottavino/(h/c), written for Colin Booth

Daniel L. Laumans (1972-), https://geelvinck.nl/kunstenaars/daniel laumans-componist
Mosella – Praeludium (1 + 2) (2008), 4', BB^b-e^{b3}, c', IMSLP
Variations romantiques pour Clavier (2013), 10', C-e^3, c [includes *bebung*], IMSLP
African Asylum: 7 Dances (2013), 10', C-e^3, clavier, IMSLP
Passacaglia in F minor (2014), 3', F-c^3, IMSLP

Dominique Lawalrée (1954-2019)
Sans entendu (1982), 10', c, first performance by Andrew de Masi (1990)

Douglas Leedy (1938-2015)
The Leaves be Green, Harmonie Universalle (1975), 6', h/c, meantone temperament advised

Ton de Leeuw (1926-1996)
Mo-Do (1974), Donemus (1975), 6', D-c^3, amplified c/h, dedicated to Annette Sachs, first performance by Annette Sachs (1974)

Nicola LeFanu (1947-), https://www.nicolalefanu.com
Broadwood Bagatelles (2021), 13', c, Canon 1, Toccata 2 and Sentimental

Song recorded by Terence Charlston and Julian Perkins on Prima Facie PFCD214 (2023)
>   Arabesque - Canon 1 – Toccata 1 - Sentimental Song – Scherzo – Twilight - Bedtime Story - Canon 2, fantasia - Toccata 2 - On a Journey – From Afar

David Lesniaski (1954-)
Suite for Clavichord, American Music Center (1978), 12', c/h/p
>   Allemande – Courante – Sarabande – Passacaglia

Ernst Lévy (1895-1981), https://ernstlevy.musicaneo.com
Twelve Pieces for clavichord or piano (1956), 19', c/p
Fourteen Pieces for clavichord or piano (1957), 22', c/p
Thirteen Pieces for Clavichord (1958), 24', c
Six Pieces for clavichord (pour Susanne) (1959), 10', c/p
Six Pieces for clavichord (1960), 11', c
Four Pieces for clavichord (1961), 8', c
Piece for piano or clavichord No.20 (1964), p/c
Fantasia ricercante, Swiss Music Archives (1966), 17', p/c, dedicated to Suzanne Levy
Fantasia Breve for Piano or Clavichord (1974), 5', p/c, dedicated to Suzanne Levy
Pour le 26 Octobre de Susanne, für Klavier oder Clavichord (1976), c/p, dedicated to Suzanne Levy
Five pieces for Clavichord or Piano (1976), 11', c/p

Robert Lind
Six Short Pieces for Keyboard, Concordia Publishing House 977912, p/h/o/c

Herbert Lindholm, https://www.herbertlindholm.net
Hefaistos' Dream, Op.84 (2014), AA-f^3, 7', c and kantele (or h and harp), first performance by Pekka Vapaavuori and Silja Kallio (2014)
>   Walking on Olympus – Apollon's Rehearsal – Seikilos' Epitaph – Resurrectional Troparion – At the Iron Forge of Hefaistos – Fall

from Olympus – Escape and Wake-up

David Loeb (1939-), http://www.philmultic.com/composers/loeb.html
Prelude, Interlude and Fugue for Well-Constructed Clavichord (1966), 6', C-f^3, c, dedicated to David Plesnicar
Fantasias and Dances (1969), 14', AA-f^3, c, dedicated to Kathleen Crees
        Fantasia – Rondeau – Scherzo – Fantasia quasi Sarabande
Mists (1969), 10', GG-e^3, treble viol and c, dedicated to Dennis Nesbitt and Kathleen Crees
Six Nocturnes (1970), 9', GG-f^3, bass viola di gamba and c, dedicated to Dennis Nesbitt and Kathleen Crees
Kazejitsu (1984), 7', koto and c, dedicated to Joan Benson
Yume No Kuni Sankei (1984), 6', A-b^{b2}, shinobue and c, dedicated to Joan Benson
Autumn and the River (1985), 7', FF-a^3, c, dedicated to Joan Benson, first performance by Joan Benson (1985)
Fleetings, 10', FF-a^3, c, dedicated to Joan Benson, one version has additional first page
Four Tanzaku, 5', AA-f^3, c
Wanderings (2020), 8', AA-f^3, c, first performance by Francis Knights (2021)
Pavane and Gagliard (2021), AA-c^3, 5', c, first performance by Francis Knights (2024)

Graham Lynch (1957-), http://grahamlynch.eu
Admiring Yoro Waterfall (2001), Composer's Edition (2018), 4', D-a^2, h/c
Petenera (2005), 10', GG#-e^3, c
        Bell – The Six Strings – Dance – De Profundis
La Forêt de Mélisande (2023), 8', FF-e^{b3}, c/h/p, for Assi Karttunen

Drake Mabry (1950-), https://www.drakemabry.com
Silent Durations XI (2004), 6', C-f^3, Sheet Music Plus, c, dedicated to Marcia Hadjimarkos, first performance by Francis Knights (2019)

Radu Malfatti (1943-), http://www.radumalfatti.eu

ma vie, non?, edition wandelweiser (1999), 33', c

nonostante I, edition wandelweiser (1999), 33', c

Roderik de Man (1941-), https://en.roderikdeman.com
What's in a name? (1985), 9', c
Elongated Fingers (2017), Donemus (2018), 8', FF-f³, c, dedicated to Menno van Delft

Tera de Marez Oyens (1932-1996)
And Blind She Remained (1978), 10', c and spoken voice, percussion, dedicated to Annette Sachs, first performance by Annette Sachs (1978)

Andrew de Masi (1947-)
Seis versos sobre 'Vinieron las naciones a tu heredad' (1978), 7', c, first performance by Andrew de Masi (1979), five-octave clavichord
Cinco versos sobre 'Bendecirá al Señor en todo tiempo' (1979), 5', c, first performance by Andrew de Masi (1979), four-octave clavichord with optional viola da gamba accompaniment

Matthias Maute (1963-), https://www.matthiasmaute.com
Fantaisie I-V pour clavicorde, recorded by Alexander Weimann on Atma ACD 2 2309 (2004)

Matteo Messori (1976-), http://www.matteomessori.com
A Harpsichord in the Multiverse: Prelude and Fugue, Da Vinci Edition DV 11985 (2022), 7', E-c³, h/(c/p), 'a temperament equabile', dedicated to Aapo Häkkinen

Ken Metz, https://www.uiw.edu/chass/directory/faculty-and-staff/metz-ken.html
In Memoriam Daniel (2017), 1', d-e³, c, Daniel Blitz Clavichord Project, recorded by David Bohn on YouTube (2017)

Donal R. Michalsky (1928-1975)

Fantasies (1961), 6', F-f^3, c/(p), written for Robert Lagerquist

Paul-Baudouin Michel (1930-2020)
Parallélloide, Centre Belge de Documentation Musicale (1973), 7', c, tape
Jeanne la folle (1987), voices and instruments, amplified c; an opera

John Middleton (1944-)
Little Suite, British Music Information Centre (1965), 6', c

Jay Mollerskov
Crooked Running Water (2017), 1', C-e^2, c, Daniel Blitz Clavichord Project, recorded by David Bohn on YouTube (2017)

Nathan Mondry (1991-), https://www.nathanmondry.com
Le Duc de la Nouvelle Orléans (2017-19), 4', AA-c^3, p/c

Stephen Montague (1943-), https://stephenmontague.com
Strumin' (1975), 8', amplified c, tape

Ivan Moody (1964-2024), https://www.ivanmoody.co.uk
Passacaglia (1982), Vanderbeek & Imrie, 3', D-b^2, h/c, dedicated to Francis Stasiak
The Sea of Marmara (1998), Vanderbeek & Imrie (2013), 6', AA-c^3, h/v/c, dedicated to Sophie Yates

Robert Moran (1937-)
Basha (1983), 15', g^1-c^3, 4 amplified c

Stefan C. Müller[211]
Fantaisiestücke für ein und zwei Viertelton-Clavicorde, c
Zirkspiel, c

---

211 See Sonnleitner (2002).

Gordon Mumma (1935-), http://brainwashed.com/mumma
Eleven-note Pieces and Decimal Passacaglia, Logos Foundation (1979), h/c
Los desaparecidos (1980), c with electronics

Gerhard Münch (1907-1988)
Clavicordii tractato (1975), c

Isaac Nagao (1938-)
The Ancient City (1986), 6', h/c, dedicated to Shinzo Oura

Aspasia Nasopoulou (1972-), http://www.nasopoulou.eu
3*1 Suite (2017-19), D-e^3, 9', c, recorded by Anna Maria McElwain on YouTube (2018)
        Utopia – Rubini – Ochto
3*2 suite for historical keyboards (2017-19), c/p, suite for c, square p, fp, glass harmonica, composed for Michael Tsalka

Alex Ness (1983-)
Twenty chords for Daniel Blitz (2017), 1', C-d^2, c, for 19-note equal temperament

Günter Neubert (1936-2021), http://www.neubert-komponist.de
Zwölf Stücke für clavicord, Peters (1963), 22', c

Serban Nichifor (1954-)
Dracula's Rag (1996), 7', FF-g^3, h/c
Dracula's Rag 2.0, 1', c, written for the Fifteen Minutes of Fame project, first performance by Monica Chew (2024)

Peter Nickol (1946-), https://www.impulse-music.co.uk/peternickol
Night thoughts, 6', BB-e^3, c
Ten miniature pieces (2010), 11', C-e^{b3}, c/p
        Scale No.1 – Scale No.2 – Invention No.1 (for the right hand) –
        Waltz No.1 – Pentamery No.1 – Pentamery No.2 – Waltz No.2 –

Invention No.2 (for the left hand) – Game No.1 – Game No.2
For One (2017), 2', D-e^3, c, Daniel Blitz Clavichord Project, recorded by David Bohn on YouTube (2017)

Makiko Nishikaze, http://www.makiko-nishikaze.de
clavics – more 1 (2017), 22', amplified c and tape
clavics – more 2 (2017), 17', amplified c and tape
clavics - more 3 (2018-20), 10', electroacoustic work
clavics - more 4 (2018-20), 9', electroacoustic work
clavics - more 5 (2018-20), 7', electroacoustic work

Carl Nielsen (1965-1931), https://www.carlnielsen.dk
In un boschetto trovai pastorella (1930), 4', D-f^3, soprano, c/p, from incidental music to the festival play *Amor og Digteren* (1930), CNW23, by Sophus Michaëlis

Walter Niemann (1876-1953)
Westminster, Eine kleine Hausmusik nach William Byrd (1913), c, violin, cello and glockenspiel

Per Nørgård (1932-)
Turn (1974), Wilhelm Hansen WH29677 (2002), 10', c, dedicated to Annette Sachs, first performance by Annette Sachs (1978), also versions for harpsichord and for piano
Three Beings (1979), Wilhelm Hansen WHKP00355 (1979), 9', FF-f^3, k, written for Eva Nordwall
      Being Beauteous – Being a Pony-Ram – Being Unpredictable

Josef Novotny, see Katharina Klement

Janet Oates, http://www.janetoates.co.uk
Humming Suite (2021), 5', c-e^3, c with vocalization, dedicated to Francis Knights, first performance by Francis Knights (2021)
      absent-mindedly – wondering – listening – self-soothing

Kris Oelbrandt (1972-), https://krisoelbrandt.nl
Micrologica 5-8, Op.32 (2012), Donemus D 13389 (2014), 4', F-e^3, c, four meditations alternating with recited poems

Nicholas O'Neill (1970-), http://www.nicholasoneill.com
Winding Down (2017), 1', F-a^2, c, Daniel Blitz Clavichord Project, recorded by David Bohn on YouTube (2017)

William Ortiz-Alvarado (1947-), https://williamortiz.com
Quodlibet (1989), c/h, first performance by Andrew de Masi (1990)

Walter Pach (1904-1977)
Toccata für Clavichord (1950), c, dedicated to Susi Jeans

Mary Lou Paschal (1937-)
Suite on the Augmented Fourth for Clavichord (1985), 5', c, dedicated to Karen Hudson-Brown, first performance by Karen Hudson-Brown (1988)
      Toccata – Sarabande – Gigue

Michael Parsons (1938-)
Clavichord Variations, c, dedicated to Pekka Vapaavuori
Oblique Piece 11, c

Akmal Parvez
Mustard Blossoms, 1', c, written for the Fifteen Minutes of Fame project, first performance by Monica Chew (2024)

Thierry Pécou (1965-), https://brahms.ircam.fr/en/thierry-pecou
Petit livre pour clavier (excerpts): Coucous, Ricercare II, 5', c, recorded by Alexandre Tharaud on Harmonia Mundi HMC 901974 (2008)

Jorge Manuel Rosado Marques Peixinho (1940-1995)
Mémoires-Miroirs (1980), 18', amplified clavichord, string orchestra,

dedicated to Annette Sachs, first performance by Annette Sachs (1980)

Craig A. Penfield (1948-)
Ricercari for Keyboard (2012), Zimbel Press 80101322, k/p/h/o/c/harmonium

Barbara Pentland (1912-2000)
Little Scherzo (1937), c, first performance by Snjolang Sogurdson (1938)

Ernst Pepping (1901-1981)
Sonate 1 (1937), Schott ED 2584 (1937), 17', GG-e^3, p, 'für mein Klavichord'

Mats Persson (1943-), http://mats-persson.se
Khroma (2006), first performance by Joel Speerstra (2006), recorded by Mats Persson on Compunctio CompCD008 (2013)
Rust, recorded by Mats Persson on Compunctio CompCD008 (2013)

Christoph Peter (1927-1982)
Für Veronika zum 15.8.1979: Präludium für Clavichord (oder Klavier, Cembalo) (1979), c/p/h

Barry Phillips, http://www.barryphillipsmusic.com
Little Pieces for Clavichord #1-7 (2014-19), 13', C-c^3, c, dedicated to Chris Campau and Joan Benson

Adrien Pièce (1988-), https://www.adrienpiece.com
Adagio (2019), 2', C-b^{b2}, c/p, IMSLP
A Pavan (2022), 3', F-f^2, c/h, IMSLP

Daniel Pinkham (1923-2006), https://composers.com/composers daniel-pinkham
Memento, ECS Publishing 5898 (2001), 2', D-d^{b3}, c, dedicated to Virginia Pleasants

Bells, ECS Publishing 5945 (2001), 2', BB-c^2, c, dedicated to Virginia Pleasants

Robert Platz (1951-)
Einstimmiges (1972-74), Gotthard F. Döring MD4097 (1974), 8', c, optional electronics

David Plesnicar (1942-), https://www.rhpp.de
Seven Canons with Prelude, Hollyhock Studios (1972), 8', h/c/o, dedicated to Jairus B. Barnes, Terry Krapenc, Steve, Bibsy and Carla Bartes, Steve, Bibsy and Matthew Bartes, Don and Paula, Dale Howard Smith, David Gooding and Emily Forsythe Warren

Hans Poort (1954-)
Berg: for clavichord and tape (1986), Donemus (1990), 12', c and tape

Beryl Price (b.1912)
Five pieces for Clavichord or Piano, Stainer & Bell 5460 (1959), C-d^3, c/(p)
    Fantasia – Preamble – Bagatelle – Promenade - Fughetta

Marta Ptaszynska (1943-), http://www.martaptaszynska.com
Soirée snobe chez la princesse (1979), c, p, acting, dedicated to Annette Sachs

Jan Raas
The Well-Frettered Clavichord (2009),[212] 3', C-d^3, c, dedicated to Koen Vermeij

Godfried-Willem Raes (1952-), https://www.logosfoundation.org
    index-god.html
Partition, Logos Foundation (1976), 10', c, tape, slides, dedicated to Annette Sachs, first performance by Annette Sachs (1976), recorded by Andrew De Masi on Logos Publiek Domain LPD006 (2000)

---

212   Printed in *Clavichord International*, xiii/2 (November 2009).

Matti Rasilainen
Homage à D'Anglebert, 5', C#-b², c
Pinea Eterna (2016), 1', C#-b², c

Lauren Redhead (1985-), https://laurenredhead.eu
Druck (2020), 4', A-d³, c/k, first performance by Francis Knights (2021)

Konrad Rennert (1958-)
Fraktur XI - Biting Off the Soldier's Thumb oder Speak up! (If You've Got Anything to Say) (1995), 32'. c, voice, 'geräuschinstrumente, synthetische Klänge und Tonband'

Hugh Collins Rice (1962-), https://www.hughcollinsrice.com
Four Abstracts for Clavichord ([2021]), 13', FF-f³, c, dedicated to Terence Charlston

Alan Ridout (1934-1996)
Suite for Clavichord (or Piano), Stainer & Bell 5501 (1961), 10', C-e³, c/p, dedicated to Thurston Dart, recorded by Peter Dickinson on Heritage HTGCD 259 (1989)

Louis-Philippe Rivet (1965-), http://www.unacorda.fr/biographies html
Nomoi of the Great Olympian Divinities (2006), 70', C-d³, electro-acoustic fretted c, tuned in 'the enharmonic genus of the hypolydian mode', six sections recorded by Renée Geoffrion (2009)
> The Nomos of Zeus – The Nomos of Poseidon – The Nomos of Hades – The Nomos of Hera – The Nomos of Demeter –
> The Nomos of Hestia – The Nomos of Athena – The Nomos of Apollo – The Nomos of Artemis – The Nomos of Aphrodite –
> The Nomos of Ares – The Nomos of Hephaestus –
> The Nomos of Hermes – The Nomos of Dionysius

Jean-Louis Robert (1947-1979)
Clav-icar (1973), 12', amplified c, dedicated to Annette Sachs, first performance by Annette Sachs (1974)
L'horizon des eaux (1976), 21', amplified c, orchestra, dedicated to Annette Sachs, first performance by Annette Sachs (1976)

Timothy Roberts (1953-)
The Fractal Ground (2023), 6', 2 c, version for two clavichords, recorded by Terence Charlston and Julian Perkins on Prima Facie PFCD214 (2023)

Jerome Roche (1942-1994)
Fantasia, Op.18 (1966), 7', C-d^3, c, dedicated to Christopher Hogwood

Theodore Rodriguez, http://msudenver.academia.edu
    TeodoroRodriguezdePacheco
Taoist Priest in Prayer, 3', G-d^3, c

Juan Luis de Pablo Enriquez Rohen (1971-), https://casatx.org
    members/juan-luis
One Cosmic Clavichord in Space, 1', c, written for the Fifteen Minutes of Fame project, first performance by Monica Chew (2024)

Claude-Robert Roland (1935-)
Sonance I, Op.18, Centre Belge de Documentation Musicale (1959), 2', c

Manuel de Roo (1979-), http://www.manuelderoo.net
Weberngedenken (2005), 1', G-c#^{3}, c

Alisa Rose, https://www.arosefiddle.com
November, 1', c, written for the Fifteen Minutes of Fame project, first performance by Monica Chew (2024)

Griffith Rose (1936-2016), https://composers.com/griffith-rose
Two Humoresques (1958), 3', F-b^2, c, dedicated to Joan Benson

Kevin Rose, http://kevinrosemusic.com
The Given Time (2017), 2', E♭-e³, c, Daniel Blitz Clavichord Project, recorded by David Bohn on YouTube (2017)

Kees Rosenhart (1939-), https://www.keesrosenhart.com
Lamento (2010), 2', C-g², c, In memoriam Nelly van Ree Bernard

Valerie Ross (1978-)
Soliloquy (2011), 5', D-c³, c, first performance by Francis Knights (2011)

Witold Rudziński (1913-2004), https://polishmusic.usc.edu/research composers/witold-rudzinski
Proverbia Latina (1974), 10', c, dedicated to Annette Sachs, first performance by Annette Sachs (1975)

Wim de Ruiter (1943-)
Zonder titel, Donemus (1986), 10', c

Heiner Ruland (1934-2017)[213]
Präludium und Fuge (1966), c
Sonatine I (1970), c
Sonatine II (1979), c
Ein Zyklus von 12 Umspielen und Reihen (1982-99), c
Sieben Üb- und Spielstücke zu den Wochentagen (1985), c
Studie in der 8 Schlesinger'schen Tönen (1988), c

Phil Salathé, http://philsalathe.com
Revanche: A Fragment (2017), 1', C#-g#², c, Daniel Blitz Clavichord Project, recorded by David Bohn on YouTube (2017)

---

213 See Sonnleitner (2002).

Dieter Salbert (1932-2006)
Chámsa - 5 Gesten, Musikverlag Zimmermann, violin and c

Bogusław Schäffer (1929-2019)
aSa (1973), 14', amplified c, dedicated to Annette Sachs, first performance by Annette Sachs (1974)

Nissim Schaul, https://www.nissimmusic.org
Small Rooms, for amplified clavichord and optional Bluetooth speakers (2018), amplified c and optional speakers, graphic score

Friedrich Schenker (1942-2013)
Ombre de Michelangelo (1984), c

Josh Schmidt, http://fortytwofootforward.com
Pieces for clavichord (2017), 20', C-f^3, c/(celesta/h/p/bayan), for David Bohn, individual movements dedicated to Brian Mani, Sarah Day, Dick Scanlan, Laura Gordon, Maggie Jo Langs, David Hartig and Summer Lee Jack

> Prelude – First Invention – Chorale – Second Invention – Touch Piece/Anthem of the Time – Waltz – Third Invention – Lullaby – Air/Tabula Rasa – Fourth and Final Invention – Post/Prelude

Prelude (for Summer Lee Jack) (2017), 1', c1#-c#^{3}, c, Daniel Blitz Clavichord Project, recorded by David Bohn on YouTube (2017)

Gunter Schneider (1954-)
wohnen (1994), 9', c 'mit Präparierung'

Martin Max Schreiner (1950-), https://webcomposer4.wordpress.com
Hops, Skips and a Jump (2017), 1', C-f^3, c, Daniel Blitz Clavichord Project, recorded by David Bohn on YouTube (2017)

Peter Schuback (1947-), http://www.peterschuback.com
Risonanzi di Euridici, I, Swedish Music Information Centre (1988), 12', c,

first performance by Kristine Scholz (1989), two versions

Anthony Scott (1911-2000)
Adagio for two clavichords (1960), 2 c, recorded by Michael Thomas and Mary Verney on Record Society RSX 16
Prelude and Fugue (1960), 4', c, dedicated to Michael Thomas, recorded by Michael Thomas on Record Society RSX 16

Cyril Scott (1879-1970), http://www.cyrilscott.net
Pastoral, c

Mátyás Seiber (1905-1960)
Pezzo per il clavicordo (1951), Schott ED 14051 (2021), 4', D-e^3, c, dedicated to Susi Jeans, first broadcast performance on 29 May 1959[214]

Rudi Seitz, https://rudiseitz.com
Canons on Clavichord, 18', c, recorded by Matthew McConnell on Bandcamp (2018)
> Celestine – Sphene – Tungsten – Amber – Spinel – Carnelian – Garnet – Ruby – Coral

Jee Seo (1985-), https://www.kco.la/composers/jee-seo
Echo, 1', c, written for the Fifteen Minutes of Fame project, dedicated to Monica Chew, first performance by Monica Chew (2024)

Gordon Sherwood (1929-2013)
Concerto grosso, Op.12 (1963), 2 violins, 2 violas, 2 cellos, c, orchestra

Tomasz Sikorski (1939-1989)
Afar a Bird (1981), c, voice, tape, dedicated to Annette Sachs, first performance by Annette Sachs (1983)

---

[214] Alastair Mitchell, *A Chronicle of First Broadcast Performances of Musical Works in the United Kingdom, 1923-1996* (Aldershot, 2001).

Tiffany M. Skidmore (1980-), www.tiffanymskidmore.com
Prelude II, B minor (2001), 2', C#-g#^{2}, c/p/h/o
Fugue II, B minor (2001), 2', E#-a^2, c/p/h/o

Denis Smalley (1946-)
Chanson de Geste, 17', c, voice, percussion, recorded by Denis Smalley (clavichord/voice), Carol Plantamura (voice/percussion) and Douglas Docherty (percussion assistant) on UEA 81063 (1979)

Andrew Martin Smith (1984-), https://www.andrewmartinsmith.com
Length/Time^2 (2017), 1', F#-e^2, c, Daniel Blitz Clavichord Project, recorded by David Bohn on YouTube (2017)

David Jason Snow (1954-), https://davidsnowmusic.org
Le Tombeau de M. Satie (2017), 1', E-g^1, c, Daniel Blitz Clavichord Project, recorded by David Bohn on YouTube (2017)

Juan Maria Solare (1966-), https://www.juanmariasolare.com
Cameo (2017), 1', A^b-d^3, c, Daniel Blitz Clavichord Project, recorded by David Bohn on YouTube (2017)

Johann Sonnleitner (1941-)[215]
Musik zum Märchen 'Das Eselein' für Traversflöte und Clavichord (1999), flute, c
Eine Beispiel-Smmlung alter Musik, zur Einfuhrung in das erweiterte Tonsystem, c

Mateo Soto (1972-), https://www.mateosoto.es
Praeludium (2017), Musica Concertata (2017), 1', A-c^3, c, Daniel Blitz Clavichord Project, recorded by David Bohn on YouTube (2017)

José Jesus de Azevedo Souza (1967-)
Reflection on the Name of DAniEl Daniel Blitz Clavichord Project (2017), 1',

---

215   See Sonnleitner (2002).

BB#-e³, c, Daniel Blitz Clavichord Project, recorded by David Bohn on YouTube (2017)
Landscape for clavichord solo, 1', c, written for the Fifteen Minutes of Fame project, first performance by Monica Chew (2024)

Burkhard Stangl (1960-), http://stangl.klingt.org
Konzert für Posaune und 22 Instrumente (1993), Random Publishing (1994), 35', trombone, instrumental ensemble, c

Krzysztof Stasiak (1962-)
Mouse Songs (1991-92), 11', E^b-c#³, c, dedicated to Francis Knights, first performance by Francis Knights (2017)
       Games – Outdoor Song – In the Shadows – Sad Song –
       Mouse Toccata
Ten Pieces (2008), 8', C-c#³, c
Four Miniatures on Polish Folksongs (2008), 3', D-b², c, first performance by Francis Knights (2024)
Three Pieces in Hungarian style, 2', D-e², c

Ekaterina Steppe (1986-)
Sky Ohm, 5', AA-e³, c

Daniel Stickan, https://stickan.org
Wassermusik: Eine Kantate über die Schöpfung, Aggregatzustände und das Mysterium der Trinität, Carus Verlag 1226200 (2023), 45', speaker, children's choir, percussion, k (p, o, ad lib c, Chor-Orgel), Geräusche

Robert Still (1910-1971)
Suite for Clavichord (1960), 8', E-d^{b3}, c, dedicated to Michael Thomas, recorded by Michael Thomas on Record Society RSX 16

Andrew Stiller (1946-)
Metric Displacement and Shibaraimono Trope of 'The Well-tempered Clavier', Praeludium I, C major (1979), Kallisti Music (1994), 6', c/h 'or other non-

sustaining keyboard instrument'

Neil Stipp (1953-), https://www.neilstipp.com
Bicinium (2017), 1', C-b^{b2}, c, Daniel Blitz Clavichord Project, recorded by David Bohn on YouTube (2017)

Karlheinz Stockhausen (1928-2007), http://www.karlheinzstockhausen.org
Tierkreis (Zodiac) (1975), c/p

Carl Stone (1953-), https://www.rlsto.net
Busobong (1980), c and electronics

Robert Anton Strobel, https://www.robertantonstrobel.com
Miniature Canon (2017), 1', c-g^2, c, Daniel Blitz Clavichord Project, recorded by David Bohn on YouTube (2017)

Aurel Stroë (1932-2008), https://www.aurelestroe.com
Anamorphoses canoniques (1984), instrumental ensemble, c and tape
Pièces pastorales (1978), 28', c and o, dedicated to Annette Sachs, first performance by Annette Sachs and Annick Rongveaux (1981)

Giles Swayne (1946-), https://gilesswayne.com
Suite, British Music Information Centre (1965), 8', c, score lost

Jadwiga Szajna-Lewandowska (1912-1994)
z miniatury (1978), c, dedicated to Annette Sachs

Jason Taurins (1991-), https://jasontaurins.com
Bagatelle (2017), 1', B-e^3, c, Daniel Blitz Clavichord Project, recorded by David Bohn on YouTube (2017)

Geoffrey Allan Taylor, https://geoffreyallantaylor.wordpress.com
Dreamscape: 'Ill met by moonlight' (1987), 10', c/h/o

Nativity Suite (1987-89, rev. 2007)
Belfry: 'A Musical Offering' (1988-94), 40', 2 p/2 k
Nativity (1992-98, rev. 2006), 20', p/c/h/o
Tamara's Tabbies (2001), 12', p/c
Pages from Homer (2004), 10', FF-f^3, c, also version with optional 2nd clavichord
Arcadian Inventions (2007), 12 , c

John Patrick Thomas (1941-), www.johnpatrickthomas-composer.com
Eloge 2 (1995), 5', FF#-f^3 (one optional f#^{3} to be played 'if possible'), c, In memoriam Thomas Walker (1936-1995), dedicated to John Whitelaw

Jude Thomas, https://composerjude.com
Fox – Wolf – Hound, 8', GG-a^{b2}, k, for ¼-comma meantone

Kurt Thomas (1904-1973), http://www.kurtthomas.de
Erste kleine hausmusik, Op.33a, Breitkopf & Härtel 5684 (1938), 8', recorder and c/h/p

Peter Thorne (1955-), https://colchesternewmusic.wordpress.com
      members/peter-thorne
Dap Dap Da Da Dap (2016), 3', F-c^3/G-c^3, 2 h/c, recorded by Terence Charlston and Julian Perkins on Prima Facie PFCD214 (2023)

Neil Thornock, https://music.byu.edu/directory/neil-thornock
Ciphered Vocalic (2017), 1', C-d^3, c, Daniel Blitz Clavichord Project, recorded by David Bohn on YouTube (2017)

Tan Tiag Yi, https://www.cssingapore.org/tan-tiag-yi
And then the Bell Tolls... (2017), 2', C#-f^3, c, Daniel Blitz Clavichord Project, recorded by David Bohn on YouTube (2017)

Gabriele Toia, http://www.musicavatar.org/avatars/gabrieletoia-libero
      it/index.html

Tamutmutef, 8', FF-f³, unfretted c, equal temperament, recorded by Eija Virtanen (2018), Gabriele Toia (2019) and Anna Maria McElwain (2022) on YouTube

Péter Tornyai (1987-), https://petertornyai.com/en
Fantasie per (tre) tastiere (2014), 13', c, spinet, electric organ, recorded by Dóra Pétery on YouTube (2014)

Julia Usher (1945-)
Clavicle (2004), alternative version *Clavicle Unstrung* (2014), 13', C-f³, fretted c/c, written for Ruby Reid-Thompson, first performance by Michaela Schmitz (2007), recorded by Andrea Gregori on Primavera DVD (2007)

André Van Belle (1943-2003)
Les miroirs du silence (1974), 10', amplified c, dedicated to Annette Sachs, first performance by Annette Sachs (1975)
Le tombeau de Marco, c, percussion, first performance by Annette Sachs (1977)

Annette Vande Gorne (1946-)
Faisceaux (1985), c/p and tape

Päivi Vartija
Sarja klavikordille (Suite for Clavichord), 10', GG-e³, c
      Preludio – Notturno – Polacca – Fuga – Finale

Ary Verhaar (1900-1994)
Muziek voor clavichord of clavicimbel (1960), Donemus 02474 (1962), 12', c/h
      Prelude – Aria – Caprice – Canon – Bourdon

Carl Vine (1945-), http://www.carlvine.com/cgi-bin/index.cgi
Everyman's Troth (1978), 20', c/(p), viola, cello, choreographed by

Don Asker, first performance by Sydney Dance Company, Carl Vine (clavichord) (1978)

Frederic Voorn (1962-), http://www.fredericvoorn.nl
Ainigma (2018), 10', GG-f^3, c/p

Anna Vriend (1961-)
Brano, 1', c, written for the Fifteen Minutes of Fame project, first performance by Monica Chew (2024)

Alexander Wagendristel (1965-), http://www.composers21.com
        compdocs/wagendra.htm
URSPRUNGZEUGNIS, für gemischten Chor und verstärktes Klavichord, Op.79 (1999), 7', choir, amplified c

Daniel Waitzman (1943-)
Sonata in F Major for Clavichord, Fortepiano, Harpsichord, or Pianoforte (2017), c/fp/h/p
Fantasia in G major for fortepiano, harpsichord, pianoforte, clavichord, or tangentflügel (2018), 13', fp/h/p/c/tangent piano, dedicated to Mrs Mona Louise Good Waitzman

David Edgar Walther, https://www.davidedgarwalther.com
Gigue for Clavichord (2023), 1', c, written for the Fifteen Minutes of Fame project, first performance by Monica Chew (2024)

Peter Walton (1953-)
In the Park (2017), 1', D-e^3, c, Daniel Blitz Clavichord Project, recorded by David Bohn on YouTube (2017)

Michael Blake Watkins (1948-)
Psallein (1971), Novello (1973), 11', instrumental ensemble (guitar solo, guitar ensemble, 2 treble guitars, 3 guitars, 1 bass guitar, 2 percussion), amplified c, first performance by Omega Players (1972)

Stephen Watkins (1954-), https://sym-phony.uk
Divisions for Clavichord (2020), 6', BB^b-e^{b3}, c, written for Francis Knights, first performance by Francis Knights (2020)

Walter Webber (1893-1977)
Air and variations, c/o, dedicated to Susi Jeans

Christoph Weinhart (1958-)
Fragmentenfantasie (2021), Edition Dohr 17541 (2023), 4', C-f^3, c, dedicated to Theresa Hagmeyer

Héloïse Werner (1991-), https://heloisewerner.com
a many-layered object (2021), 9', AA^b-f3/FF-f^3, 2 c, recorded by Terence Charlston and Julian Perkins on Prima Facie PFCD214 (2023)

Willyn Whiting, https://www.willynwhiting.com
Corals, 1', c, written for the Fifteen Minutes of Fame project, first performance by Monica Chew (2024)

Blair Whittington
99 (2017), 1', E-f^3, c, Daniel Blitz Clavichord Project, recorded by David Bohn on YouTube (2017)

Christopher Wicks (1975-), http://www.societyofcomposers.org/members/ChristopherWicks
The Temptation of Orpheus, Op.627 (2017), 1', C#-e^{b3}, c, Daniel Blitz Clavichord Project, recorded by David Bohn on YouTube (2017)

Thom Willems (1955-), https://www.boosey.com/composer/Thom+Willems
Verteldgung der Wölfe (1978), 6', c and voice, first performance by Annette Sachs

Manon-Liu Winter, http://manonliuwinter.at
MM (2005), 5-60', c and electronics
7 lost words (2011), 2 c, bass recorder, viola da gamba

Haimo Wisser (1952-1998)
Durchdringungen, Vier Sätze für Klavichord (1988), 11', c, first performance by Peter Waldner (1995)

Peter Witchell (1945-), https://www.composersalliance.com composers/index.cfm?composer=180
Denny's Sequel: A Little Suite for Clavichord (1986), 7', c, first performance by Nicholas Reed (1986)
    Lady Upmarket's Route March (with rests) – The Tartan Twitch – Mrs. Mack's Misery – Gentry's Jigge

Peter Wolf (1942-)
Saltarelle hongroise (1971), Éditions musicales Tutti (1971), 3', c, oboe, bassoon, percussion

James Woodman (1957-)
Warde's Dump, 3', c, recorded by Timothy Broege on Allaire (2016)
Gagliarda for Emily and Kip, 2', c, recorded by Timothy Broege on Allaire (2016)

Roger Zahab (1957-), https://www.music.pitt.edu/people/roger-zahab
New Gardens, No.6 from *Eight moments* (2014), A-a^2, c, for Valerie Strong and George Faddoul

Alfred Zimmerlin (1955-), http://alfredzimmerlin.ch
Clavierstück 4 (1992), 2-6', c/k, first performance by Jean-Jacques Dünki (1992)

John Zorn (1953-)
Shibboleth (2005), violin, viola, cello, percussion, c, recorded by Stephen Drury on Tzadik 8035 (2007)

SELECT DISCOGRAPHY

This select list of LP and CD recordings including contemporary clavichord music provides a guide to some of the material that is available.[216] Entries are indexed alphabetically by performer, and the data for each recording is arranged in four lines, indicating the following:

Title (duration)
Music content
Instrument(s)
Format, Label, recording and date

The title is given in italics if it represents the actual cover title of the disc; otherwise, it is descriptive. A prefatory asterisk indicates that the recording also includes non-clavichord items, which are not listed here. This is followed by the total disc or set timing, rounded to the minute. The recording contents are normally given in the original order where known, in a standardized format. Composers are separated by semi-colons, and works by commas. Minor keys are shown in lower case, with sharps and flats indicated '#' and 'b'. The instrument maker, model and date are listed, with a superscript letter system used to key this to the contents where more than one instrument appears. The format of the recording is preceded by the number of items in a set, where larger than one, followed by the record label, series name (where relevant), number, recording date and (P) date. Thus '2 CD Prima Facie PFCD065/66, recorded 2016, (P) 2017' indicates a two-CD set issued by Prima Facie with the number PFCD065/66, recorded in 2016 and and published in 2017. Editorial additions are given in square brackets.

---

216   For a complete discography, see Knights (2020).

Due to the ever-changing nature of the record catalogues, and the fragmented international nature of the market, availability is not always easy to determine, and label distributors and current catalogue status are therefore not given here. The second-hand market, including online retailers and auction companies, is a useful source for some rare material.

TIMOTHY BROEGE

New and old music for clavichord (70')
Howells: De la Mare's Pavan, Sir Hugh's Galliard (from *Lambert's Clavichord*); Harrison: Sonatas Nos.1 and 5 (from *Six Sonatas*); Persichetti: Sonatinas Nos.5 and 6; C. P. E. Bach: Sonatinas Nos.3 and 4 (*Sechs neue Clavier-Stücke*, Wq.63.9-10). La Gleim, Wq.117/19; Hovhaness: Dark River and Distant Bell; Woodman: Warde's Dump, Gagliarda for Emily and Kip; Kosinksi: Prisms; Broege: The Sad Pavane, Sonatas Nos.1 and 2 (from *Five Sonatas*), Fantasia for clavichord, Partita for clavichord, Paws for a moment
Carl Fudge (1985) after J. C. G. Schiedmayer (1796)
CD Allaire [no number], recorded 2015, (P) [2016]

TERENCE CHARLSTON and JULIAN PERKINS

Chit Chat – Music for Two Clavichords (64')
Peter Thorne: Dap Dap Da Da Dap; Maxwell Davies: Four Lessons for Two Keyboards, Op.81; Farewell to Stromness; Héloïse Werner: a many-layered object; Iain Farrington: Chit Chat 2020; Nicola LeFanu: 3 pieces from Broadwood Bagatelles; Terence Charlston: Five Pieces for Two Clavichords; Timothy Roberts: The Fractal Ground; Alexander J. Blustin: Idle thoughts of owls
Peter Bavington (2002) after attrib Johann Heinrich Silbermann (c.1775), Andreas Hermert (2020) after Johann Emanuel Schön (1748)
CD Prima Facie PFCD214, rec 2023, (P) 2023

ANDREW DE MASI

Godfried-Willem Raes: 4 Others (64')
Raes: Partition
Joris Potvlieghe
CD Logos Publiek Domain LPD006

PETER DICKINSON

Blue Clavichord (78')
Dickinson: Suite for the Centenary of Lord Berners, 5 Diversions;
Ridout: Suite; Hoddinott: Sonatina, Op.18; Ellington arr Dickinson: In a sentimental mood, Don't get around much anymore, Prelude to a kiss, Sophisticated Lady, It don't mean a thing
Hugh Gough single-strung (c.1957)
CD Heritage HTGCD 259, recorded 1989, issued c.2012

JEAN-JACQUES DÜNKI

Tétraclavier (65')
Dünki: Tétraptéron 0-IV [with Paul Clemann (piano), Stéphane Reymond (harpsichord), Pierre Subiet (celesta)]
Gerrit Klop (1981)
CD Jecklin JS 289-2, recorded 1992, (P) 1993

Pour le clavier (67')
Dünki: Andere kindestücke (1960-2002), Cinq études pour le clavichorde (1990-2012), Zwei studien (2004)
Thomas Steiner (2006) after Christian Gottlob Friederici (1773)
CD Pianoversal PV 102, recorded 2013, (P) 2018

RUTH DYSON

Howells and the Clavichord
Howells: Lambert's Clavichord Op.41; Goff's Fireside, Patrick's Siciliano, Dyson's Delight, Ralph's Pavan and Galliard, Finzi's Rest, Berkeley's Rest, Walton's Toye (from *Howells' Clavichord*)
Thomas Goff (1934)
LP Wealden Prestige WS 194, recorded 1981, (P) 1981

RENÉE GEOFFRION

Louis-Philippe Rivet, Extraits du Nomoi of the Great Olympian Divinities (18')
Rivet: The Nomos of Aphrodite, The Nomos of Hephaestus, The Nomos of Hermes, The Nomos of Dionysius, The Nomos of Hades, The Nomos of Zeus
Renée Geoffrion after Anon Austrian
CD [no label or number], recorded 2009, (P) 2009

LUTZ GERLACH

*Liese rieselt der Schnee
Lutz Gerlach: Fragile
Sperrhake
CD LGM, (P) 2010

*Fragile: 22 Miniaturen für clavichord
Lutz Gerlach: Fragile
Sperrhake
CD LGM, (P) 2010

KEITH JARRETT

The Book of Ways (101')
Jarrett: The Book of Ways *The Feeling of Strings*

Merzdorf
2 CD ECM 831 396-2 and 1344/45, recorded 1986, (P) 1987

JEROEN MALAISE

Jeroen Malaise: Keyboard Works Part 1 (67')
Malaise: La Follia Mediterranea
Joris Potvleighe (2018) after Jacob Adlung (1726)
CD Et'cetera KTC 1690, recorded 2020, (P) 2020

PAMELA NASH

Gary Carpenter: Die Flimmerkiste, Works for Ensemble (70')
Carpenter: Van Assendelft's Vermeer
Peter Bavington (1999)
CD NMC Records D111, recorded 2006, (P) 2007

MAKIKO NISHIKAZE

clavichords harpsichords (59')
Nishikaze: clavics-more
Andreas Hermert
CD Coviello Classics COV 92114, (P) 2021

JULIAN PERKINS

Dialogues: The Music of Stephen Dodgson, Volume 2 (59')
Dodgson: Suite No.1 in C, Suite No.2 in E$^\flat$
Karin Richter (1998) after Christian Gottlob Hubert (1771)
CD Campion Cameo 2088, recorded 2008, (P) 2009

Herbert Howells: Complete Clavichord Works (86')
Howells: Lambert's Clavichord Op.41: Howells' Clavichord
Arnold Dolmetsch (1925), Thomas Goff (1952), Peter Bavington (2005)

after attrib Johann Heinrich Silbermann (c.1775)
2 CD Prima Facie PFCD065/66, recorded 2016, (P) 2017

MATS PERSSON

Klavikord (59')
Elköf: Nodes No.1-7; Persson: Khroma, Rust; Elköf and Persson: Blue Bell, Bole, Teal, Icterine [with Andreas Elköf (zither)]
Pehr Lundborg (1778), Lindholm & Söderstrom (1808), Ragnar Köhlin (1996)
CD Compunctio CompCD008, recorded 2012, (P) 2013

LUDGER SINGER

Mediterra Nova (72')
Singer: Platz des himmlichen Flieders, Flamenco techno, Lusitanisches Tagebuch, Fashion, Gaze and Pyre, Sketches of Rain, Tanz der Wampentiere, Die Zen Gebote, Mediterra Nova, New Derek-tions for Clavichord, Hans Dampf in San Alberto, Make Five, Monitor aus, Herr Pastor trifft Herrn Schneider, Schon vorbei, Touch my Hall, Lämse (Bonus Blues)
Ludger Singer (c.1980, *flügelförmiges* clavichord)
CD Luxaries LUX 34000/3, recorded 1995-97, (P) 1997
Syntopia (62')
[Trio Delight: Albrecht Maurer (violin), Meike Herzig (recorder, fujara), Ludger Singer (clavichord, didgeridoo)]
Ludger Singer (c.1980, *flügelförmiges* clavichord)
CD Classical Music Network CMN 001, recorded 2000, (P) 2001

MICHAEL THOMAS

Works for Clavichord and Harpsichord
Anthony Scott: Adagio (with Mary Verney, clavichord); Robert Still: Suite; Anthony Scott: Prelude and Fugue; Lennox Berkeley: Prelude and Fugue

Op.55/3; Eugene Goossens: Forlane and Toccata
[mono 10" 33rpm] Record Society RSX 16

JAROSLAV TŮMA

A Portrait of Clavichord (126')
Graupner: Suite in C (Ouverture, Chaconne, Entrada); J. S. Bach: French Suite No.6 in E BWV 817; C. P. E. Bach: Rondo II in c Wq.59/5, Fantasia I in F Wq.59/4; Štěpán: Sonata in E^b; Mozart: Variations on Ah, vous dirai-je, Maman K265; Howells: Lambert's Clavichord, Op. 41; J. S. Bach arr Tůma: Chaconne in d BWV1004
Johann Christoph Georg Schiedmayer (1787)
2 CD, Arta F10241, recorded 2019, (P) 2019

MANON-LIU WINTER

10. Komponistenforum Mittersill 8.–17. September 2005
2 CD Ein Klang Records Nr.018/019, rec 2005, (P) 2005

BIBLIOGRAPHY

Anon, 'Mr. Hipkins's Lecture on "The Old Claviers"', *The Musical Times and Singing Class Circular*, xxxi/574 (1 December 1890), pp.719-722.

_____, 'Music in Edinburgh', *The Musical Times and Singing Class Circular*, xxxviii/647 (1 January 1897), p.31

_____, 'President Roosevelt Greatly Interested in Clavichord', *The Music Trades* (26 December 1908), p.9.

_____, *Dolmetsch and his Instruments* (Haslemere: Arnold Dolmetsch, 1929).

_____, 'The British Clavichord Society Awards for Clavichord Composition', *British Clavichord Society Newsletter*, 27 (October 2003), pp.22-23

_____, 'Discovery of an "English" clavichord', *British Clavichord Society Newsletter*, 60 (October 2014), pp.38-40.

_____, 'A nineteenth-century harpsichord promoter, with a famous music collection, who had dealings with Arnold Dolmetsch', https://www.semibrevity.com, accessed 24 May 2024.

Derek Adlam, 'Arts and Crafts and the Clavichord, The Revival of Early Instrument Building in England', in Brauchli, Brauchli and Galazzo (1996), pp.201-212.

_____, Review of 'Bach: *Preludes, Fantasies & Fugues*, Peter Sykes (clavichord)', *British Clavichord Society Newsletter*, 61 (February 2015), pp.27-30.

Christian Ahrens and Gregor Klinke (eds.), *Fundament aller Clavirten Instrumenten — Das Clavichord*, 2001 Herne symposium proceedings (Munich and Salzburg, 2003).

Robert Anderson, 'Howells and the Clavichord', *The Musical Times*, cxxiii/1667 (January 1982), pp.35-36.

Cornelia Auerbach, *Die deutsche Clavichordkunst des 18.Jahrhunderts* (Kassel: Bärenreiter, 1930).

Antonio Baldassarre, 'Forgotten in plain sight: Anti-Semitism, identity, and music, a portrait of Ernst Levy (1895-1981)', in Marinković et al. (2018), pp.188-244.

John Barnes, 'The Parallel between the Harpsichord and Clavichord Revivals in the Twentieth Century', in Brauchli, Brauchli and Galazzo (1995), pp.233-240.

_____, 'Hugh Gough, 1916–1997', *British Clavichord Society Newsletter*, 8 (June 1997), p.24.

Brandon Bascom, *The legacy of József Gát on piano performance and Pedagogy*, DMA dissertation (University of Iowa, 2012).

Peter Bavington, 'Thomas Goff and his Clavichords', *British Clavichord Society Newsletter*, 16 (February 2000), pp.7-11.

_____, 'The British Clavichord Society Awards for Clavichord Composition, 2004', *British Clavichord Society Newsletter*, 30 (October 2004), pp.20-23.

_____, 'Technical Drawings of Clavichords', in Wardman (2005), pp.53-61

_____, '20th- and 21st-century music for the clavichord', *British Clavichord Society Newsletter*, 38 (June 2007), pp.3-10.

_____, 'Tom Goff by Himself', *British Clavichord Society Newsletter*, 39 (October 2007), pp.31-32.

_____, 'Arnold Dolmetsch's clavichord making in the years before 1914', in Brauchli, Galazzo and Wardman (2008), pp.45-58.

_____, 'Clavichords in Britain No. 13: The Arnold Dolmetsch clavichord in St Cecilia's Hall, Edinburgh', *British Clavichord Society Newsletter*, 42 (October 2008), pp.3-8.

_____, 'Clavichord and Shakuhachi (performance of Yumi Hara Cawkwell, Nota Bene, by Kiku Day and Michael Bonaventure)', *British Clavichord Society Newsletter* 44 (June 2009), pp.8-9.

_____, 'Clavichords in Britain, No.17: The Arnold Dolmetsch Clavichord at Fenton House' *British Clavichord Society Newsletter*, 56 (June 2013), pp.7–11.

_____, 'A Clavichord by Herbert Lambert', *British Clavichord Society Newsletter*, 58 (February 2014), pp.3–16.

_____, 'Restoration of a Chickering/Dolmetsch clavichord', *Clavichord International*, xv/2 (November 2011), pp.42-46.

_____, 'Advice for Post-War Clavichord Constructors', *British Clavichord Society Newsletter*, 61 (February 2015), pp.41-43.

_____, Jürgen Ammer and the Ammer Dynasty', *British Clavichord Society Newsletter*, 69 (October 2017), pp.4-10.

_____, 'Obituary: Wolfgang Joachim Zuckermann (1922–2018)', *British Clavichord Society Newsletter*, 73 (Spring 2019), pp.28-29.

_____, 'The Chickering-Dolmetsch Early-Instrument Log-Book: An Introduction', *The Consort*, lxxix (2023), pp.61–104.

_____, 'Henry Tull, an unsung hero of the harpsichord and clavichord revival', *Harpsichord & Fortepiano*, xxviii/2 (Spring 2024), pp.14-28.

Frances Bedford, 'The Historical Significance of Harpsichord Compositions Written Between 1913 and 1928', *American Music Teacher*, xxii/4 (1973), p.25.

_____ and Robert Conant, *Twentieth Century Harpsichord Music: A Classified Catalog* (Hackensack, N.J.: J. Boonin,1974).

_____, *Harpsichord & Clavichord Music of the Twentieth Century* (Berkeley: Fallen Leaf Press, 1993).

_____, 'Twentieth Century Clavichord Music', in Brauchli, Brauchli and Galazzo (1994), pp.259–264.

Lothar Bemmann, 'The Decline and Revival of the Clavichord', in Brauchli, Galazzo and Moody (2004), pp.29-36.

_____, 'The Clavichord in Films', in Brauchli, Galazzo and Wardman (2006), pp.249-258.

_____, 'The Harmony died away; The Elusive Clavichords of Gottfried Silbermann, Part II', *Clavichord International*, xix/1 (May 2015), pp.12-19 at 12.

_____, trans. Gregory Crowell, 'Further to "The Harmony died away"; The Elusive Clavichords of Gottfried Silbermann', *Clavichord International*, xxii/2 (November 2018), pp.58-61.

Joan Benson, 'The Clavichord in 20th Century America', in Maria Fernanda Cidrais Rodrigues, Manuel Morais and Rui Vieira Nery (eds.), *Livro De Homenagem a Macario Santiago Kastner* (Lisbon: Serviço de Música, 1992).

_____, 'Clavichord Technique in the mid-twentieth century', in Brauchli, Brauchli and Galazzo (1994), pp.255-257.

_____, 'Clavichord Perspectives from Goethe to Pound', in Brauchli, Galazzo and Moody (2004), pp.139-147.

_____, 'Piano to Clavichord (1925-1962)', *Clavichord International*, x/2 (November 2006), pp.38-41.

_____, 'Twentieth-Century Music' in Igor Kipnis (ed.), *The Routledge Encyclopedia of Keyboard Instruments, II: Harpsichord and Clavichord*, (London: Routledge, 2007), p.78.

Eric Blom, 'Bach and the Clavier', *The Musical Times*, lxix/1019 (1 January 1928), pp.25-27.

Donald Boalch, rev. Charles Mould, *Makers of the Harpsichord and Clavichord* (Oxford: Oxford University Press, 3/1995), now online at https://boalch.org.

Erwin Bodky, 'Clavichord Music from 1500-1800', *Bulletin of the American Musicological Society*, xi-xiii (September 1948), pp.28-29.

Maria Boxall, 'The Origins and Evolution of Diatonic Fretting', *The Galpin Society Journal*, liv (May 2001), pp.143-199.

Bernard Brauchli, 'A Comprehensive List of Iconographical Documents on the Clavichord', in Brauchli, Brauchli and Galazzo (1994a), pp.81–92, supplemented in successive volumes of this series.

_____, *The Clavichord* (Cambridge: Cambridge University Press, 1994b).

_____, Susan Brauchli and Alberto Galazzo (eds.), *De Clavicordio* (Turin: Musica Antica a Magnano, 1994).

_____, Susan Brauchli and Alberto Galazzo (eds.), *De Clavicordio II*, Proceedings of the

International Clavichord Symposium (Turin: Musica Antica a Magnano, 1995).

_____, Susan Brauchli and Alberto Galazzo (eds.), *De Clavicordio III*, Proceedings of the International Clavichord Symposium (Magnano: Musica Antica a Magnano, 1997).

_____, Alberto Galazzo and Ivan Moody (eds.), *De Clavicordio V*, Proceedings of the International Clavichord Symposium (Magnano: Musica Antica a Magnano, 2002).

_____, Alberto Galazzo and Ivan Moody (eds.), *De Clavicordio VI*, Proceedings of the International Clavichord Symposium (Magnano: Musica Antica a Magnano, 2004).

_____, Alberto Galazzo and Judith Wardman (eds.), *De Clavicordio VII*, Proceedings of the International Clavichord Symposium (Magnano: Musica Antica a Magnano, 2006).

_____, Alberto Galazzo and Judith Wardman (eds.), *De Clavicordio VIII*, Proceedings of the International Clavichord Symposium (Magnano: Musica Antica a Magnano, 2008).

_____, Alberto Galazzo and Judith Wardman (eds.), *De Clavicordio IX*, Proceedings of the International Clavichord Symposium (Magnano: Musica Antica a Magnano, 2010).

_____, Alberto Galazzo and Judith Wardman (eds.), *De Clavicordio X*, Proceedings of the International Clavichord Symposium (Magnano: Musica Antica a Magnano, 2012).

Timothy Broege, 'What Makes It "Clavichord" (or not)?', *Tangents*, xl (Spring 2016), p.1.

G. A. Briggs (ed.), *Audio Biographies* (Bradford: Wharfedale Wireless Works, 1961).

Garry Broughton, 'The Clavichord and Affairs of State (and Jazz)', *British Clavichord Society Newsletter*, 35 (June 2006), pp.21-22.

_____, 'Bruckner's Clavichords', *British Clavichord Society Newsletter*, 65 (June 2016), pp.3-5.

_____, 'Bruckner's Clavichords', *Bruckner Journal*, xxii/2 (July 2018), pp.17-18.

_____, 'Did Picasso Play the Clavichord?', *British Clavichord Society Newsletter*, 74 (Summer 2019), pp.3-6.

Peter Brownlee, 'Remembering Joan Benson', *Harpsichord and Fortepiano*, xxv/1 (Autumn 2020), pp.21–27.

Alan Bullard, http://www.alanbullard.co.uk/clavichord-music/ (2019), accessed 14 June 2024.

Margaret Campbell, *Dolmetsch: the man and his work* (London: Hamilton, 1975).

Nellie Chaplin, 'The Harpsichord', *Music and Letters*, iii/3 (July 1922), pp.269-273.

Joel Cohen and Herb Snitzer, *Reprise: The Extraordinary Revival of Early Music* (Boston: Little, Brown, 1985).

Dalyn Cook, 'Lotta Van Buren: Pioneering Performer, Educator, and Restorer', *Clavichord International*, xxiii/1 (May 2019), pp.7-10.

Gregory Crowell, 'Victor Hammer and the Revival of the Nineteenth-Century Clavichord', in Brauchli, Galazzo and Wardman (2012), pp.53–62.

_____, 'Isolde Ahlgrimm and the Historical Clavichord', *Clavichord International*, xiii/2 (November 2009), pp.58-59.

_____, 'Clavichord Customers at Chickering & Sons, 1906–1914', *Clavichord International*, xvi/2 (November 2012), pp.42-46.

Mads Damlund and Joris Potvlieghe, 'Carl Nielsen and the Clavichord', *Clavichord International*, xix/2 (November 2015), pp.55-61.

Mads Damlund, 'Carl Nielsens clavichord', *Organistbladet* (February 2016).

_____, 'Two letters from Carl Nielsen', *Clavichord International*, xxiii/1 (May 2019), pp.17-20.

Thurston Dart (ed.), *Clavichord Music of the Seventeeth Century* (London: Stainer & Bell, 1960).

Willem Derks, *The harpsichord in the twentieth century* (Leeuwarden: Sybren Hellinga Stichting, 1994).

Saviola Diadorim and Maria Pia Jacobini, *Il Clavicembalo nella Musica Contemporanea Italiana, Catalogo e Ricerca* (Bologna: Associazione clavicembalistica bolognese, 2005).

Gerhard Doderer and John Henry Van der Meer, *Cordofones de tecla portugueses do século XVIII: Clavicórdios, Cravos, Pianofortes e Espinetas* (Lisbon: Fundação Calouste Gulbenkian,

2005).

Gerhard Doderer, 'The Clavichord in Portugal after 1800', in Brauchli, Galazzo and Wardman (2008), pp.75-90.

Arnold Dolmetsch, *The Interpretation of The Music of the XVII and XVIII Centuries* (London: Novello and Co., 1916).

Carl Dolmetsch, '*Plus fait douceur que violence*: Arnold Dolmetsch and the Clavichord', *The Consort*, lii/2 (Autumn 1996), p.101.

Mabel Dolmetsch, *Personal Recollections of Arnold Dolmetsch* (London: Routledge & Paul, 1957).

'Dotted Crotchet', 'The Musical Library of Mr. T. W. Taphouse, M. A.', *The Musical Times*, xlv/740 (1 October 1904), pp.629-636.

Jessica Douglas-Hume, *Violet: The Life and Loves of Violet Gordon Woodhouse* (London: Harvill Press, 1996).

Carl Dudash, 'An Upright Clavichord', *Clavichord International*, xiii/1 (May 2009), pp.21-24.

Jean-Jacques Dünki, 'Tetrapteron, A Keyboard Quartet: The Difficulty of Integrating the Sounds of Piano, Harpsichord, Celesta and Clavichord', in Brauchli, Brauchli and Galazzo (1995), pp.249-253.

_____, 'Composing "with" the Clavichord — A Contemporary Experience', in Brauchli, Brauchli and Galazzo (1997), pp.277-282.

Martin Elste, *Modern Harpsichord Music: A Discography* (Westport, CT: Greenwood Press, 1995).

Enciclopedia universal ilustrada europeo-americana (Madrid: Espasa-Calpe S.A., 1908-1930).

Carl Engel, *A descriptive catalogue of the musical instruments in the South Kensington Museum* (London: G. E. Eyre and W. Spottiswoode, 1874).

_____, 'Some Account of the Clavichord with Historical Notices', *The Musical Times and Singing Class Circular*, xx/439 (1 September 1879), pp.468-472.

Karrin Ford, 'The Pedal Clavichord and the Pedal Harpsichord', *The Galpin Society Journal*,

1 (1997), pp.161–179.

Sally Fortino, 'Clavichord Music with Extended Tonality: a report from Switzerland', *British Clavichord Society Newsletter*, 53 (June 2012), pp.8-9.

Hubert J. Foss, 'Herbert Howells: A Brief Survey of His Music', *The Musical Times*, lxxi/1044 (1 February 1930), pp.113-116.

James Gardner, 'Interview with Peter Owen', *The Sunday Feature* (8 May 2016).

Renée Geoffrion, 'The Electro-Acoustic Clavichord', *Tangents*, xvii (Fall 2004), pp.1, 5-6.

Bruce W. Glenny, 'Herbert Howells: Aspects of Twentieth-Century English Revivalism as seen in "Lambert's Clavichord"', in Brauchli, Brauchli and Galazzo (1996), pp.225-231.

Thomas Goff, ['Interview'], in Briggs (1961), pp.144-149.

_____, 'Violet Gordon Woodhouse – Her Playing of the Clavichord', in Douglas-Home (1996), pp.320-327.

Franz August Göhlinger, *Geschichte des Clavichords* (Basel: Buchdruckerei E. Birkhäuser, 1910).

George Grove (ed.), *A dictionary of music and musicians*; Appendix, ed. J. A. Fuller Maitland (London: Macmillan, 1889).

Herbert Grundhewer and Lothar Bemmann, *Musik für Clavichord aus dem 20. und 21. Jahrhundert, Bibliografie* (Berlin: Deutschen Clavichord Societät, 2023).

Tim Hamilton, 'A Very Small Dolmetsch', *Tangents*, xviii (Spring 2005), pp.4-5.

_____, 'Clavichord Labeled M. J. Schramm, München', *Tangents*, xxi (Fall 2006), pp.6-7.

R. A. Hands, 'A Scientific Approach to the Clavichord', *The Galpin Society Journal*, xx (March 1967), pp.89-98.

Edmund Handy, 'A Profile of the Modern Clavichord', *British Clavichord Society Newsletter*, 13 (February 1999), pp.3-7.

Harry Haskell, *The Early Music Revival: A History* (London: Thames and Hudson, 1988).
Katharine Hawnt. '*Strange Luggage*': Raymond Russell, the Harpsichord and Early Music Culture

in the Mid-Twentieth Century, PhD thesis (University of Southampton, 2021).

Christine Hedinger, 'Kurt Hessenberg's "Zehn Kleine Präludien", Op.35, for Piano or Clavichord', in Brauchli, Brauchli and Galazzo (1997), pp.283-286.

Eva Helenius-Öberg, *Svenskt klavikordbygge 1720-1820: studier i hantverkets teori och praktik jämte instrumentens utveckling och funktion i Sverige under klassisk tid* (Stockholm: Almqvist & Wiksell International, 1986).

Eva Helenius, 'Aspects of the Clavichord in Sweden in the Nineteenth Century', in Brauchli, Galazzo and Wardman (2006), pp.45–62.

Uta Henning, 'Arnold Dolmetsch and his Bach Clavichord: an Iconographical and Literary Approach', in Brauchli, Galazzo and Wardman (2008), pp.17-25.

Arthur J. Hipkins, 'Carl Engel's Clavichords', *The Musical Times and Singing Class Circular*, xx/439 (1 September 1879), p.492.

_____, 'The Old Clavier or Keyboard Instruments; Their Use by Composers, and Technique', *Proceedings of the Musical Association*, 12th Session (1885-1886), pp.139-148.

_____, 'A Lecture on Spinets, Harpsichords, and Clavichords. Read in the Music Room of the International Inventions Exhibition, October 21 and 23, 1885', *The Musical Times and Singing Class Circular*, xxvi/513 (1 November 1885), pp.646-649.

_____, *A Description of the History of the Pianoforte and of the Older Stringed Keyboard Instruments* (London and New York: Novello, 1896, 3/1929).

Christopher Hogwood (ed.), *Fitt for the Manicorde: A seventeenth-century English collection of keyboard music* (Launton: Edition HH, 2003).

Peter Holman, 'The harpsichord in 19th-century Britain', *Harpsichord & Fortepiano*, xxiv/2 (Spring 2020), pp.4-14.

Herbert Howells, arr. Alan Ridout, *Miniatures for Organ* (Rattlesden: Kevin Mayhew, 1993).

Frank Howes, *The English musical Renaissance* (New York: Stein and Day, 1966).

Edgar Hunt, 'A Harpsichord Odyssey (1)', *The English Harpsichord Magazine*, ii/8 (April 1981), pp.190-194.

Richard Ireland, 'Thomas Goff Clavichord Number One Discovered', *British Clavichord Society Newsletter*, 24 (October 2002), pp.8-12.

Philip James, 'The Clavichord', *The Musical Times*, lxxvi/1106 (April 1935), pp.319-321.

Susi Jeans, 'The Pedal Clavichord and Other Instruments of Organists', *Proceedings of the Royal Musical Association*, 77th session (1950–51), pp.1–15.

Harry Joelson, 'The Thirteen Clavichords of Henry Schumacher', *Clavichord International*, vii/1 (May 2003), pp.4-12.

Jean-Théo Jiolat, Jean-Loïc Le Carrou and Christophe d'Alessandro, 'Whistling in the Clavichord', *HAL open science*, hal-03947709v1 (2022).

Edmond Johnson, 'The Death and Second Life of the Harpsichord', *The Journal of Musicology*, xxx/2 (Spring 2013), pp.180-214.

Joseph R. Jones, 'The Clavichord in the Bluegrass', *Clavichord International*, xiv/2 (November 2010), pp.45-50.

Douglas Keislar, 'History and Principles of Microtonal Keyboards', *Computer Music Journal*, xi/1 (Spring 1987), pp.18-28.

Linda S. Khadavi, *Twentieth-Century Harpsichord Music: Selected Playing Techniques*, DMA dissertation (University of Missouri-Kansas City, Missouri, 1983).

Yae Ji Kim, *The Clavichord Revival in England, the U.S., and Finland: A Dialog with the Modern Piano*, PhD thesis (Sydney Conservatorium of Music, 2019).

Ralph Kirkpatrick, 'On Playing the Clavichord', *Early Music*, ix/3 (July 1981), pp.293-305.

_____, *Early years* (New York: Peter Lang, 1985).

_____, ed. Meredith Kirkpatrick, *Letters of the American Harpsichordist and Scholar* (Rochester, NY: University of Rochester Press, 2014).

_____, ed. Meredith Kirkpatrick, *Reflections of an American Harpsichordist* (Rochester, NY: University of Rochester Press, 2017).

Francis Knights, 'Johann Sebastian Bach und das Clavichord: Argumente für ein verkanntes Instrument', *Neue Zeitschrift für Musik* (November 1990), pp.15-18.

_____, 'Some Observations on the Clavichord in France', *The Galpin Society Journal*, xliv (1991), pp.71-76.

_____, 'Composing for the Clavichord', in Wardman (2005), pp.9–10.

_____, 'Exploring Chopin on the clavichord', *Tangents*, xlv (October 2019), pp.1-4.

_____, *Clavichord Discography* (Hebden Bridge: Peacock Press, 2/2020).

_____, 'Early keyboard duets', *Sounding Board*, xvi (2021), pp.21-33.

_____, 'Modern music for the virginals', *Sounding Board*, xvii (2021), pp.51-54.

_____, 'Early Music in the Novel', *Dolmetsch Foundation Bulletin*, New Series No.40 (Autumn 2021), pp.9-11.

_____, 'An index of early keyboard makers', *National Early Music Association Newsletter*, vi/1 (Spring 2022), pp.126-136.

_____, 'A bibliographic guide to women pioneers of the harpsichord', *Sounding Board*, xviii (April 2022), pp.73-81.

_____, 'The evolution of modern clavichord music', in Rebecca Cypess, Esteli Gomez and Rachel Lansang (eds.), *Historical Performance and New Music: Aesthetics and Practices* (Abingdon: Ashgate, 2024), pp.106-117.

John Koster, 'Hugh Gough', *The Galpin Society Journal*, li (July 1998), pp.7-9.

Edward L. Kottick, *A History of the Harpsichord* (Bloomington: Indiana University Press, 2003).

Mark Kroll (ed.), *The Cambridge Companion to the Harpsichord* (Cambridge: Cambridge University Press, 2019a).

_____, *The Boston school of harpsichord building: Reminiscences of William Dowd, Eric Herz and Frank Hubbard by the people who knew and worked with them* (Hillsdale, NY: Pendragon Press, 2019b).

Herbert Lambert, *Modern British composers: seventeen portraits by Herbert Lambert* (London: F. & B. Goodwin, 1923).

Christopher Lewis, *The Harpsichord in Twentieth-Century Britain*, PhD thesis (University of Southampton, 2017).

Laurence Libin, 'Clavichords at Vassar College', *Harpsichord & Fortepiano*, xxvii/2 (Spring 2023), pp.20-25.

Joyce Lindorff, *Contemporary Harpsichord Music: Issues for Composers and Performers*, DMA dissertation (Juilliard School of Music, New York, 1982).

Chau-Yee Lo, *Endangered Species: The Harpsichord and its New Repertoire since 1960*, PhD thesis (University of Leeds, 2004).

J. A. Fuller Maitland and William Barclay Squire (eds.), *The Fitzwilliam Virginal Book* (Leipzig: Breitkopf & Härtel, 1894-99).

Sonja Marinković, Vesna Mikić, Ivana Perković, Tijana Popović Mladjenović, Ana Stefanović and Dragana Stojanović-Novičić (eds.), *Challenges in Contemporary Musicology: Essays in Honor of Prof. Dr. Mirjana Veselinović-Hofman* (Belgrade: Faculty of Music, 2018).

Jane Marlin, *Reminiscences of Morris Steinert* (New York: G. P. Putnam's sons, 1900).

Richard George Marshall, *The Career and reputation of Herbert Howells*, MA thesis (University of Durham, 2005).

Katharine May, 'Obituary: Francis Haward Clarke', *British Clavichord Society Newsletter*, 13 (February 1999), pp.13-15.

Anna Maria McElwain, 'A Clavichordist's View of the Chopin Preludes', unpublished paper (Sibelius Academy, 2010).

_____, 'VII Nordic Historical Keyboard Festival', *National Early Music Association Newsletter*, ii/2 (July 2018), pp.82–86.

Thomas McGeary, 'Michael Thomas (1922–2022): an anniversary tribute', *Harpsichord & Fortepiano*, xxvii/2 (Spring 2023), pp.4-11.

Eckehart and Susanne Merzdorf, *Merzdorf; 100 Janhre Cembalobau* (Neulingen: J. S. Klotz, 2020).

Lynne Mirrey, 'Pioneers of the English Clavichord-playing Revival: 1. Dorothy Swainson', *British Clavichord Society Newsletter*, 36 (October 2006), pp.2-6.

———, 'Pioneers of the English Clavichord Revival, 2: Herbert Lambert', *British Clavichord Society Newsletter*, 41 (June 2008), pp.8–14.

Alastair Mitchell, *A Chronicle of First Broadcast Performances of Musical Works in the United Kingdom, 1923-1996* (Aldershot: Ashgate, 2001).

Kenneth Mobbs, 'The BCS at Haslemere, September 1995: the work of Arnold Dolmetsch', *British Clavichord Society Newsletter*, 4 (February 1996), pp.11-13.

John Morley, 'Fifty Years of Clavichord Making: Robert Morley and Co.', *British Clavichord Society Newsletter*, 32 (June 2005), pp.2-5.

Ian Mortimer, 'Rex Muffett (1927-2004): Teaching the clavichord', *British Clavichord Society Newsletter*, 31 (February 2005), pp.25-28.

Charles Mould, 'An Index of British Makers of Historical Keyboard Instruments', *The Galpin Society Journal*, xix (April 1966), pp.101-130.

Hanns Neupert, *Das Klavichord* (Kassel: Bärenreiter, 1948), trans. Ann P. P. Feldberg, *The Clavichord* (Kassel: Bärenreiter, 1965).

Walter Niemann, *Das Klavierbuch, kurze Geschichte d. Klaviermusik u. ihrer Meister, d. Klavierbaues u. d. Klavierliteratur* (Munich: Callwey Verlag, 1907).

Jenny Nex and Lance Whitehead, 'The six early clavichords of Arnold Dolmetsch: their construction and inspiration', *The Galpin Society Journal*, liii (2000), pp.274-300.

Christopher Palmer, *Herbert Howells: a study* (Sevenoaks: Novello, 1978).

Larry Palmer, 'Herbert Howells' "Lambert's Clavichord"', *Diapason*, xii (December 1974), pp.7–8.

———, 'Some Literary References to the Harpsichord and Clavichord, 1855-1923', *Diapason*, lxiv (September 1983), p.18.

———, *Harpsichord in America: A Twentieth Century Revival* (Bloomington: Indiana University Press, 1989).

_____, 'Contemporary Harpsichord Music', in Kroll (2019), pp.324-346.

John Paul, *Modern harpsichord makers* (London: Gollancz, 1981).

Keith Paulson-Thorp, *The Twentieth-Century Harpsichord: Approaches to Compositional and Performance Practices as Evidenced by the Contemporary Repertoire*, PhD dissertation (University of Illinois, Urbana-Champaign, 1981).

Rita Pieretti, 'Contemporary Clavichord Music in Italy', in Brauchli, Brauchli and Galazzo (1994), pp.264-266.

Lionel Pike, 'Flights of Fancy: Codes and Keys in Howells', *Tempo*, lxii/244 (April 2008), pp.11-18.

Stewart Pollens, *A history of stringed keyboard instruments* (Cambridge: Cambridge University Press, 2022).

Olga Poltoratskaya, 'A guide to clavichord kits', *Tangents*, xiv (Spring 2003), pp.3-8.

Martin Pühringer, '"Jaras me hizo 1858" — das jüngste aller Clavichorde?', in Ahrens and Klinke (2003), pp.155-165.

Dollie Radford, *A Ballad of Victory and other Poems* (London: Alston Rivers, 1907).

John Rawson, 'Thomas Goff: some memories', *British Clavichord Society Newsletter*, 40 (February 2008), pp.28-30.

Forrest Read (ed.), *Pound/Joyce: The Letters of Ezra Pound to James Joyce with Pound's Essays on Joyce* (New York: New Directions, 1967).

Huw Rees, 'The Hohner clavinet', *Clavichord International*, xvii/1 (May 2013), pp.6-13.

Edwin M. Ripin, 'A Reassessment of the Fretted Clavichord', *The Galpin Society Journal*, xxiii (August 1970), pp.40-48.

Raymond Russell, 'The Harpsichord since 1800', *Proceedings of the Royal Musical Association*, 82nd Session (1955-1956), pp.61-74.

Howard Schott, 'The Harpsichord Revival', *Early Music*, ii/2 (April 1974), pp.85-95.

_____, 'From Harpsichord to Pianoforte: A Chronology and Commentary', *Early Music*, xiii/1 (February 1985), pp.28-38.

_____, 'The Clavichord Revival, 1800-1960', *Early Music*, xxxii/4 (November 2004), pp.595-603.

Paul Simmonds, 'The BCS Awards for Clavichord Composition', *British Clavichord Society Newsletter*, 27 (October 2003), pp.22-23.

_____, 'The Story of a Pantalon Clavichord', *Clavichord International*, xi/1 (May 2007), pp.22-26.

_____, 'Carl Engel and the Clavichord', *The Galpin Society Journal*, lxi (April 2008), pp.105-113.

_____, 'The Carl A. Pfeiffer Piano Company', *Clavichord International*, xvii/1 (November 2013), pp.34-41.

_____, 'What the Label does not tell us: Further Thoughts on Clavichords from the Pfeifer Workshop', in *Clavichord International*, xix/1 (May 2015), pp.20–27.

_____,'Pfeiffer/Marx Clavichords: A Postscript', *Clavichord International*, xxii/1 (May 2018), p.24.

Florian Sonnleitner, 'The Klavikantal - A new Type of Clavichord in Development', in Brauchli, Galazzo and Moody (2002), pp.73-76.

Johann Sonnleitner, 'The Clavichord in the Expanded Tone System', in Brauchli, Galazzo and Wardman (2002), pp.63–71.

Joel Speerstra, *Bach and the Pedal Clavichord: an Organist's Guide* (Rochester, NY: University of Rochester Press, 2004).

Paul Spicer, *Herbert Howells* (Bridgend: Border Lines, 1998).

Michael Steinberg, 'Some Observations on the Harpsichord in Twentieth Century Music', *Perspectives of New Music*, i/2 (Spring 1963), pp.189-194.

Christopher Stembridge, 'Obituary: David Bolton', *British Clavichord Society Newsletter*, 41 (June 2008), pp.31-32.

Lyndon Johann Taylor, 'The Case for and against the Electric Clavichord', *British Clavichord Society Newsletter*, 8 (June 1997), pp.7–10.

———, 'Reconstructing Silbermann's Cembal d'Amour', *Clavichord International*, i/2 (November 1997), pp.43-45.

Richard Runciman Terry, [Review of Lambert's Clavichord], *The Spectator* (7 November 1928).

Michael Thomas, 'Modern Music for the Clavichord', *The Consort*, xviii (1961), pp.96–102.

———, 'The Fretted Clavichord', *The English Harpsichord Magazine*, i/2 (April 1974), pp.39-47.

Ruby Reid Thompson, 'Twentieth-Century Music for the Clavichord', *British Clavichord Society Newsletter*, 9 (October 1997), pp.8–9.

Gwendolyn Toth, *Twentieth-Century Solo Harpsichord Music in the Kirkpatrick Collection of the Library of the Yale School of Music*, MMA dissertation (Yale University, New Haven, 1981).

Peter Tracton, 'Turnabout is Fair Play or Repertoire Theft for Fun and Profit', *Tangents*, xx (Spring 2006), p.5.

Richard Troeger, 'The Dolmetsch/Chickering Clavichords and their Model', in Brauchli, Brauchli and Galazzo (1996), pp.213-224.

———, 'Landowska and the Clavichord', *Harpsichord & Fortepiano*, xix/1 (Autumn 2014), pp.7–8.

Rosalyn Tureck, 'Bach: Piano, Harpsichord or Clavichord', *American Music Teacher*, xi/3 (January-February 1962), pp.8-9, 30.

———, 'Bach in the Twentieth Century', *The Musical Times*, ciii/1428 (February 1962), pp.92-94.

Luk Vaes, 'Extraordinary Sounds and Techniques in Friedrich Wilhelm Rust's Sonata in G', *Clavichord International*, xvii/1 (May 2013), pp.14–23.

Rob van Acht (ed.), *Harpsichords, Clavichords, Organs, Harmoniums: Checklists of the musical instrument collection of the Haags Gemeentemuseum, The Hague* (The Hague: Haags Gemeentemuseum, 1989).

Marie van Rhijn, 'Reflections on Stephen Dodgson's Clavichord Suites', *British Clavichord Society Newsletter*, 68 (June 2017), pp.13-14.

Koen Vermeij, 'Eighteenth-Century Lovers of the Clavichord: Which Makers did They Prefer?', in Brauchli, Brauchli and Galazzo (1995), pp.105-114.

Lavern Wagner, 'The Clavichord Today', *Periodical of the Illinois State Music Teachers Association*, vi/1 (Spring 1968), pp.20-38 and 'The Clavichord Today, Part II', vii/1 (Summer 1969), pp.1-16.

Martin John Ward, *Analysis of five works by Herbert Howells, with reference to features of the composer's style*, MPhil thesis (University of Birmingham, 2005).

Judith Wardman, 'Thomas Goff and his Clavichords: a brief introduction', *British Clavichord Society Newsletter*, 15 (October 1999), pp.18-20.

_____, 'A Concert for Haward Clarke, Hampstead, 10 October 1999', *British Clavichord Society Newsletter*, 16 (February 2000), pp.6-7.

_____ (ed.), *International Clavichord Directory* (London: British Clavichord Society, 2/2005).

_____, 'Clavichord recital by Geoffrey Allan Taylor', *British Clavichord Society Newsletter*, 39 (October 2007), pp.10-11.

_____, 'Women Harpsichordists and the Clavichord: some observations', *Sounding Board*, xviii (April 2022), pp.58-72.

Harold E. Watts, 'Bach's "48": Use of the Pedal, and Other Problems', *The Musical Times*, lxxx/1160 (October 1939), pp.722-724.

John Weston, 'George Bernard Shaw and the Clavichord: Part 3', *British Clavichord Society Newsletter*, 19 (February 2001), pp.15-18.

Lance Whitehead, 'Clavichords in Britain No.9: The 1894 Dolmetsch at the Royal College of Music', *British Clavichord Society Newsletter*, 21 (October 2001), pp.8-11.

Norman Wilkinson, 'A note on the clavichord and the harpsichord', *Music and Letters*, iv/2 (April 1923), pp.162-169.

Nick Wilson, *The Art of Re-enchantment: Making Early Music in the Modern Age* (Oxford: Oxford University Press, 2014).

Ilton Wjuniski, 'The Twelve Sonatas by Friedrich Wilhelm Rust Published by Vincent d'Indy and their Performance on the Clavichord', in Brauchli, Galazzo and Wardman (2010), pp.101–105.

Peter Wolf, 'Reminiscences of Three Performers and an Instrument Maker', *Bach*, xlviii/2-xlix/1 (2018), pp.21-43.

Joseph Wörsching, *Die historic Saitenklaviere und der moderne Clavichord- und Cembalo-Bau* (Mainz: Rheingold-Verlag, 1946).

H. E. Wortham, 'Lambert's Clavichord', *The Sackbut*, ix/6 (March 1929), pp.278-279.

Wolfgang Zuckermann, *The Modern Harpsichord: Twentieth-Century Instruments and their Makers* (New York: October House, 1969).

INDEX

Ackroyd, Poppy 73
Adlam, Derek 42
Ahlgrimm, Isolde 34
Albrechtsberger, Johann Georg 13
Alcalay, Luna 37, 74
Allen, Hugh 50
Allen, Kevin 74
Al-Sawad, Muhammad-Adam 48, 74
Alter, Aaron 75
Ammer, Alois 25
Ammer, Michael 25
Andriamorasata, Nantenaina 74
Andriessen, Hendrik 55, 68, 75
Andriessen, Jurriaan 55, 75
Andriessen, Louis 75
Angerer, Paul 75
Aragon, Jared Isaac 75
Argent, Mark 75
Arnold, Malcolm 51
Auerbach, Cornelia 25
Aveling, Valda 37
Avni, Boaz 75

Baboukis, John 76
Bach, Carl Philipp Emanuel 22, 25, 60, 61
Bach, Johann Sebastian 3, 13, 18, 22, 23,
　　25, 31, 32, 35, 36, 38, 60
Bachmann, Nancy 76
Baggio, Rodrigo 76
Balogh, Máté 76
Bank, Jacques 37, 76
Bardwell, William 37, 76
Bares, Peter 54, 76
Barganier, Erich 77
Barnes, John 26

Barrell, Bernard 77
Barrell, Joyce 77
Bart, Nans 77
Bartók, Béla 70
Bäsecke-Beltrametti, Dennis 77
Báthory-Kitsz, Dennis 77
Baur, Jurg 42
Bebelaar, Patrick 77
Becerra-Schmidt, Gustavo 77
Beckwith, John 78
Bedford, Frances 10
Beecham, Thomas 38
Beffa, Karol 78
Bemmann, Lothar 10
Benary, Peter 78
Benson, Joan 34, 37, 53, 61
Berkeley, Lennox 46, 51, 52, 68, 78
Bernard, Robert 56, 78
Bertram, Hans Georg 78
Bibby, Gillian 58, 78
Bliss, Arthur 51
Blitz, Daniel 43
Blom, Eric 7
Blustin, Alexander J. 46, 78
Bodky, Erwin 34, 35
Boguslawski, Edward 37, 79
Bohn, David 43, 79
Bohn, James 79
Bolton, David 29
Boult, Adrian 51
Bowman, Herbert 35
Brafford, Ben 79
Brahms, Johannes 13
Branch, Erik 79
Brauchli, Bernard 60

Bream, Julian 51
Brickman, Scott 79
Bridges, Robert 5, 6
Bridgham, Meadow 79
Britten, Benjamin 38
Broadwood 35, 36
Broege, Timothy 47, 53, 61, 70, 80, 126
Brooks, John 80
Brown, Vanessa 80
Bruckmann, Ferdinand 80
Bruckner, Anton 13
Bruzdowicz, Joanna 37, 66, 80
Buchholz, Thomas 80
Bührer, Urs 81
Bullard, Alan 38, 52, 68, 81
Busoni, Ferrucio 12, 16
Butterfield, Christopher 81
Byrd, William 38

Cahn, Peter 54, 81
Cairati, Alfredo 24
Calabris, Michael 49, 81
Camp, Red 48, 73
Carey, Ross James 54, 61, 81
Carlson, Erik 82
Carpenter, Gary 42, 67, 68, 82
Casablancas Domingo, Benet 82
Castelnuovo-Tedesco, Mario 12
Cawkwell, Yumi Hara 58, 82
Chakraborty, Utsyo 82
Challis, John 17, 20, 23, 36
Chanler, Theodore 23, 53, 82
Chaplin, Nellie 18
Charles, Simon 42
Charlston, Terence 46, 60, 61, 82, 126
Chatterton, J. G. 14
Chew, Monica 43, 83
Chickering & Sons 16, 21, 33, 53
Clarke, Haward 20, 37, 38, 45, 51, 52, 53
Clayson & Garrett 26
Clements, Dominy 83

Cobby, J. C. 20
Cocchetti, D. E. 83
Cohn, James 83
Coleman, Michael 84
Cooman, Carson 47, 49, 68, 84
Coral, Leonardo 84
Cowell, Paul 85
Cranmer, John 41
Crees, Kathleen 37, 52, 53
Cunningham, Michael 85
Curran, Alvin 85

Dalton, Jim 85
Dart, Thurston 36, 45, 51, 60, 70
DaSilva, Douglas 85
Davies, Henry Walford 33
Davies, Peter Maxwell 38, 46, 47, 85
Davis, Doug 85
DeBlasio, Chris 53, 85
Debussy, Claude 70
Demi, Federico 86
DeWalt, Philip 86
de la Mare, Walter 6
de Lacour, Marcelle 12, 56
De Laet, Joris 37, 86
De Wolfe 37
Dézsy, Thomas 86
Dickinson, Peter 38, 46, 47, 49, 52, 68, 86, 127
Diederichs, Yann 37, 86
Dijk, Jan van 55, 87
Dodgson, Stephen 20, 42, 48, 52, 68, 87
Dolmetsch, Aline 3
Dolmetsch, Arnold 3, 5, 12, 13, 15, 16, 18, 21, 22, 23, 26, 27, 31, 32, 33, 36, 38, 46, 53, 56, 59, 69
Dolmetsch, Carl 3, 21, 32, 35
Dolmetsch, Elodie 32
Dolmetsch, Friedrich 3
Dolmetsch, Mabel 15, 17
Dolmetsch, Rudolph 38

Donahue, Thomas 87
Drexler, David 87
Drischner, Max 87
Dudash, Carl 6
Dudman, Colin 87
Dufy, Raoul 5
Duisberg, Robert 87
Duke, David 88
Dünki, Jean-Jacques 57, 88, 127
Durmaz, Alp 88
Duryee, Alissa 8, 9, 42, 68, 69, 89
Dyson, George 51
Dyson, Peter 52, 89
Dyson, Ruth 37, 128

Ebert, Wolfgang-Heinrich 89
Ecklebe, Alexander 37, 89
Edelan 6
Eisenbrey, Keith 89
Elia, Marios Joannou 89
El-Dabb, Halim Abdul Messieh 89
Elköf, Andreas 90
Ellenberger, Kurt 90
Engel, Carl 7, 22, 35, 36
Érard 12
Erdmann-Abele, Veit 38, 66, 90

Fagnilli, Nicholas 90
Falla, Manuel de 67
Faivre, Christian 90
Farrington, Iain 46, 90
Feldberg, John 26, 27
Fellowes, Edmund 50
Ferrari, Carlotta 90
Ferrero, Lorenzo 38, 90
Finnissy, Michael 91
Finzi, Gerald 51
Fiske, Roger 46
Forget, Philippe 42, 56, 61, 68, 91
Foss, Hubert 80
Frischknecht, Hans 91

Friederici, Christian Gottfried 13
Froberger, Johann Jacob 60
Fruehwald, Robert 91
Fukushima, Yasuharu 91
Fulkerson, James 91
Fuller Maitland, John Alexander 15, 50

Galsworthy, John 6
Ganer, Christoph 14
Gaveau 16, 33, 46, 56
Gentilucci, Marta 91
Geoffrion, Renée 9, 128
Gerlach, Lutz 128
Gerry, W. H. 6
Gershwin, George 48
Gibbens, John Jeffrey 91
Gifford, Gerald 91
Glaus, Daniel 92
Glazier, Laurence 92
Goble, Robert 17, 26, 27, 59
Goebbels, Heiner 92
Goeyvaerts, Karel 37, 55, 92
Goff, Thomas 6, 19, 20, 26, 34, 36, 38, 51, 52, 59, 60, 69, 70
Göhlinger, Franz August 25
González Acilu, Agustín 92
Goossens, Eugene 46, 92
Gough, Hugh 7, 17, 38
Grahn, Ulf 92
Grillo, Fernando 37, 92
Grove, George 15
Grundhewer, Herbert 10
Grunnert 21
Guessford, Jesse 93
Gulda, Friedrich 93
Guy, Barry 63, 65, 68, 69, 93

Haacke, Walter 47, 54, 93
Haas, Robert 70
Hadley, Patrick 51
Hallgrimsson, Haflidi 93

Hambraeus, Bengt 94
Hämeenniemi, Eero 57, 94
Hamilton, Tim 24
Hammer, Victor 17
Harburger, Walter 4, 94
Hardy, Thomas 6
Harich-Schneider, Eta 36
Harkavyy, Oleh 94
Hass 15, 18, 21, 26, 28, 32, 35
Haubenstock-Ramati, Roman 37, 63, 64, 94
Haydn, Joseph 61
Hawkins, Malcolm 37, 94
Hawksworth, John 94
Heath, Edward 38
Heathcote, James 94
Henderson, Benjamin D. 94
Henning, Karl 95
Hermert, Andreas 60
Hersom, Alex 95
Hessenburg, Kurt 54, 68, 95
Hewett, James 95
Hildreth, Nigel 37, 95
Hills, Gorman 23, 53, 95
Hipkins, Alfred James 14, 20, 35
Hipkins, Edith 20
Hoddinott, Alun 45, 52, 68, 95
Hodsdon, Alex 26, 38
Hoffman, Ferdinand 13
Hoffmann, Christian Gotthelf 16, 18, 21
Hoffmann 14
Hohner 10
Hold, Trevor 52, 96
Horne, Herbert 15
Hovhaness, Alan 96
Howells, Herbert 1, 4, 19, 38, 42, 49, 50, 51, 52, 67, 68, 69, 96
Hubert, Christian Gottlob 25, 28
Hunt, Edgar 33
Hunt, Hubert 33
Hurley, Susan 73

Ismagilov, Timur 42, 97

Jacob, Gordon 51
James, Philip 31
Jancarz, C. L. 97
Jarrett, Keith 48, 60, 73, 128
Jeans, Susi 37
Jestl, Bernhard 97
Johnson, Jane 97
Jones, Tamsin 97
Joyce, Brian 98
Joyce, James 5
Jungwirth, Rudolf 98

Kann, Hans 98
Kan-no, Shigeru 98
Karttunen, Assi 52
Kaufmann, Dieter 98
Keil, Friedrich 98
Kemper 25
Kennedy, Michael 42, 98
Kent, Duke of 20
Keys, Ivor 51
Kilpiö, Lauri 57, 98
Kipnis, Igor 37
Kirkman 18, 21
Kirkpatrick, Ralph 12, 20, 21, 22, 36, 53, 60
Klement, Katharina 54, 63, 98, 99
Knüsel, Alfred 99
Kosch, Michael 99
Kosinksi, Andrew 99
Kotschy, Johannes 100
Krämer, Johann Paul 18
Kraus, Eberhard 100
Kreutz, Alfred 34
Kullberg, Erling 57, 100
Kunz, Klemens 7
Kuronen, Jouni 100

Lacerda, Osvaldo 100
Lachert, Piotr 37, 38, 55, 100
Lagerquist, Robert 53
Lambert, John 58, 102
Lambert, Herbert 4, 19, 20, 49, 50
Landowska, Wanda 12, 21, 56
Lane, Liz 102
Laumans, Daniel L. 102
Lawalrée, Dominique 102
LeFanu, Nicola 46, 102
Leedy, Douglas 49, 102
Leeuw, Ton de 55, 102
Lemme 23
Lengemann, Fritz 8
Leonhardt, Gustav 39
Lesniaski, David 103
Lévy, Ernst 52, 56, 102
Levy-Loetscher, Suzanne 56
Ligeti, Gyorgy 67
Lind, Robert 103
Lindholm, Herbert 57, 58, 104
Liszt, Franz 13
Little, J. W. 29
Loeb, David 37, 48, 53, 61, 104
Luesser, Joseph 17
Lynch, Graham 42, 47, 52, 68, 104

Mabry, Drake 104
Maendler 25
Maendler, Karl 24
Malaise, Jeroen 129
Malcolm, George 51
Malfatti, Radu 104
Man, Roderik de 55, 105
Marez Oyens, Tera de 38, 66, 105
Martinů, Bohuslav 12
Marx, Otto 23, 24
Masi, Andrew de 105, 127
Mauger, Ed 7
Maute, Matthias 105
McElwain, Anna Maria 57

McKenna, David 19
McKenna, Pamela 19
Mendelssohn, Felix 13, 90
Merzdorf 7, 60
Messori, Matteo 48, 105
Metz, Ken 105
Michalsky, Donal R. 48, 53, 105
Michel, Paul-Baudouin 106
Middleton, John 106
Milton, John 6
Mollerskov, Jay 43, 45, 106
Mondry, Nathan 106
Montague, Stephen 106
Moody, Ivan 49, 68, 106
Moore, George 6
Moran, Robert 48, 106
Morley, John 26, 27
Morley, John Sebastian 27
Moscheles, Ignaz 31
Mould, Charles 26
Mozart, Wolfgang Amadeus 61
Muffat, Rex 70
Müller, Stefan C. 8, 106
Mumma, Gordon 106
Münch, Gerhard 107
Nagao, Isaac 107

Nash, Pamela 42, 129
Naslopoulou, Aspasia 42, 48, 107
Nesbitt, Dennis 53
Ness, Alex 49, 107
Neubert, Günter 54, 107
Neumeyer, Fritz 36
Neupert, Hanns 25
Neupert, J. C. 21, 25
Nichifor, Serban 107
Nickol, Peter 42, 52, 107
Nielsen, Carl 13, 108
Niemann, Walter 4, 108
Nishikaze, Makiko 108, 129
Nørgård, Per 38, 67, 108

Novotny, Josef 98

Oates, Janet 66, 108
Oelbrandt, Kris 109
O'Neill, Nicholas 109
Ortiz-Alvarado, William 109
Owen, Peter 20

Pach, Walter 109
Palazzi, Nicola 18
Pangritz, Andreas 39
Paris Workshop 30
Parsons, Michael 109
Parvez, Akmal 109
Paschal, Mary Lou 109
Pass, Joe 48
Pauer, Ernst 31
Paul, John 21, 26
Pécou, Thierry 109
Peixinho, Jorge Manuel Rosado Marques 38, 59, 109
Pelton Jones, Frances 16
Penfield, Craig A. 110
Pentland, Barbara 110
Pepping, Ernst 54, 68
Perkins, Julian 42, 46, 126, 129
Persichetti, Vincent 70
Persson, Mats 57, 110, 130
Peter, Christoph 110
Peterson, Oscar 48
Pfeiffer 24
Phillips, Barry 110
Pièce, Adrien 110
Pinkham, Daniel 110
Pisaurensis, Dominicus 23
Platz, Robert 110
Pleasants, Virginia 37, 41
Plesnicar, David 111
Pleyel 12
Pollens, Stewart 60
Poort, Hans 49, 111

Poulenc, Francis 67
Pound, Ezra 5, 6
Price, Beryl 45, 111
Ptaszynska, Marta 38, 111
Pyne, James Kendrick 32

Raas, Jan 111
Radford, Dollie 5
Raes, Godfried-Willem 38, 111
Rasilainen, Matti 111
Rawnsley, Sean 7
Redhead, Lauren 112
Renaissance Workshop 30
Rennert, Konrad 112
Rice, Hugh Collins 112
Ridout, Alan 45, 46, 52, 68, 112
Ripin, Edwin 8
Rivet, Louis-Philippe 9, 56, 70, 112
Robert, Jean-Louis 38, 58, 113
Roberts, Timothy 113
Roche, Jerome 113
Rodriguez, Theodore 113
Rohen, Juan Enriquez Luis de 113
Roland, Claude-Robert 113
Roo, Manuel de 113
Roosevelt, Theodore 32
Rose, Alisa 113
Rose, Griffith 48, 53, 113
Rose, Kevin 114
Rosenhart, Kees 114
Ross, Valerie 114
Rossini, Gioacchino 11
Rubbra, Edmund 51
Rudziński, Witold 38, 114
Ruiter, Wim de 114
Ruland, Heiner 8, 114
Runciman, John 16
Ruskin, John 18
Russell, Raymond 21
Rust, Friedrich Wilhelm 62

Sachs, Annette 37, 55, 63, 66
Salaman, Charles 31
Salathé, Phil 115
Salbert, Dieter 115
Samuel, Harold 50
Sargent, Malcolm 50
Sassmann 24
Schäffer, Bogusław 38, 115
Schaul, Nissim 63, 64, 115
Schenker, Friedrich 54, 115
Schiedmayer, Johann Christoph Georg 13
Schiedmayer, J. & P. 25
Schmahl 13
Schmidt, Josh 54, 115
Schmitz, Micaela 42
Schneider, Gunter 115
Schott, Howard 11
Schramm, M. J. 24
Schreiner, Martin Max 115
Schuback, Peter 115
Schumacher, Henry 36
Schütze, Rainer 27
Scott, Anthony 46, 116
Scott, Cyril 116
Seiber, Mátyás 52, 68, 116
Seitz, Rudi 116
Selbiger, Liselotte 36
Seo, Jee 116
Shaw, George Bernard 5
Sherwood, Gordon 58, 116
Shuckburgh, Evelyn 20, 70
Sikorski, Tomasz 38, 66, 117
Silbermann, Gottfried 7, 13
Simmonds, Paul 41, 42
Sinclair, Jean Stuyvesant 33
Singer, Ludger 130
Sitwell, Edith 6
Sitwell, Osbert 6
Skidmore, Tiffany M. 117
Skowroneck, Martin 27
Smalley, Denis 58, 117

Smith, Andrew Martin 117
Snow, David Jason 117
Solare, Juan Maria 117
Sonnleitner, Johann 8, 117
Soto, Mateo 117
Souza, José Jesus de Azevedo 117
Spányi, Miklós 25, 60
Speerstra, Joel 42
Sperrhake 25
Squire, William Barclay 50
Stangl, Burkhard 118
Stasiak, Krzysztof 118
Stein 24
Steinberg, Michael 10
Steiner, Thomas 60
Steinert, Morris 13, 35
Steppe, Ekaterina 118
Stickan, Daniel 93, 118
Still, Robert 46, 118
Stiller, Andrew 118
Stipp, Neil 119
Stirling, J. F. 29
Stockhausen, Karlheinz 119
Stone, Carl 49, 119
Stravinsky, Igor 70
Street, Joseph 14
Strobel, Robert Anton 119
Stroë, Aurel 38, 119
Sücka, Johann 13
Swainson, Dorothy 33, 46, 56
Swayne, Giles 119
Szajna-Lewandowska, Jadwiga 35, 119

Taphouse, Eleanor 18
Taphouse, Thomas William 18, 35
Taskin, Pascal 12, 28
Taurins, Jason 119
Taylor, Geoffrey Allan 38, 42, 119
Taylor, Lyndon Johann 7
Terry, Richard Runciman 1, 50
Thomas, John Patrick 61, 120

Thomas, Jude 49, 120
Thomas, Kurt 120
Thomas, Michael 7, 26, 33, 36, 46, 130
Thomas and Rhodes 26
Thomé, Francis 12
Thorne, Peter 46, 120
Thornock, Neil 120
Tiag Yi, Tan 120
Toia, Gabriele 42, 68, 120
Tomasini 12
Tornyai, Péter 121
Tull, Henry 19, 20
Tůma, Jaroslav 131
Tureck, Rosalyn 31, 34
Tyrwhitt, Gerald (Lord Berners) 5

Usher, Julia 42, 52, 63, 68, 121

Van Belle, André 38, 121
Van Buren, Lotta 16, 33
Vande Gorne, Annette 121
Van Delft, Menno 55
Vartija, Päivi 57, 121
Vaughan Williams, Ralph 51
Verdi, Giuseppe 11
Verhaar, Ary 121
Vermeij, Koen 28
Vierne, Louis 20
Vine, Carl 121
Volhard, Brigette 54
Voorn, Frederic 122
Vriend, Anna 122

Wagendristel, Alexander 122
Wagner, Lavern 10
Waitzman, Daniel 122
Walther, David Edgar 122
Walton, Peter 122
Walton, William 51, 70
Watkins, Michael Blake 122
Watkins, Stephen 123

Watts, Harold E. 18
Webber, Walter 123
Weinhart, Christoph 123
Werner, Héloïse 46, 63, 123
Wess, Thomas 46
Whiting, Willyn 123
Whittington, Blair 123
Wicks, Christopher 123
Wilkinson, Norman 18
Willems, Thom 55, 123
Williams, Tom 38
Winter, Manon-Liu 124, 131
Wisser, Haimo 124
Witchell, Peter 124
Wittmayer 25
Wolf, Peter 23, 124
Wolff, Charles 30
Woodhouse, Violet Gordon 6, 16, 17, 19, 34, 70
Woodman, James 124
Woolley, Dennis 26
Wörsching, Joseph 24

Zahab, Roger 124
Zimmerlin, Alfred 124
Zorn, John 124
Zuckermann 29
Zuckermann, Wolfgang 27

www.ingramcontent.com/pod-product-compliance
Lightning Source LLC
Chambersburg PA
CBHW060945170426
43197CB00025B/2997